It's Never Too Late to Be Happy

The Psychology of Self-Reparenting

It's Never Too Late to Be Happy

The Psychology of Self-Reparenting

Muriel James

Addison-Wesley Publishing Company, Inc.
Reading, Massachusetts • Menlo Park, California
Don Mills, Ontario • Wokingham, England • Amsterdam • Sydney
Singapore • Tokyo • Mexico City • Bogotá • Santiago • San Juan

Photo credits:
Ulrike Welsch, pages ii, xiv, 19, 22, 24, 45, 91, 98, 107, 113, 131, 139, 145, 185, 192, 211, 212
Frances M. Cox/Stock, Boston, page 20
Challiss Gore, pages 39, 59, 103, 139, 162, 171
Peggy Ann Bliss, pages 40, 97, 128, 149
Peter Simon/Stock, Boston, page 42
N. Fuller-Hebble, page 61
Muriel James, pages 70, 200
José Mercado, pages 81, 113
Preservation Press, pages 121, 136
Steve Karpman, page 131
Sally Johnson, page 165

Production Coordinator: BMR, San Francisco, CA
Cover design: Marshall Henrichs
Interior design: David Crossman, BMR
Typographer: Walker Graphics

Library of Congress Cataloging in Publication Data

James, Muriel.
 It's never too late to be happy.

 Includes index.
 1. Transaction analysis. 2. Happiness.
I. Title.
RC489.T7J355 1985 158'.1 85-7420
ISBN 0-201-11620-0 P

ABCDEFGHIJ-898765

OTHER BOOKS by MURIEL JAMES

Published by Addison-Wesley:

Breaking Free: Self-Reparenting for a New Life

Marriage Is for Loving

Techniques in Transactional Analysis for Psychotherapists and
  Counselors

The OK Boss

Born to Love: Transactional Analysis in the Church

Transactional Analysis for Moms and Dads: What Do You Do with
  Them Now That You've Got Them?

CO-AUTHORED with DOROTHY JONGEWARD

Born to Win: Transactional Analysis with Gestalt Experiments

Winning with People: Group Exercises in Transactional Analysis

The People Book: Transactional Analysis for Students

Winning Ways in Health Care

CO-AUTHORED with LOUIS SAVARY

A New Self: Self-Therapy with Transactional Analysis

Published by Harper & Row:

The Power at the Bottom of the Well

The Heart of Friendship

To John, Betty, and Margaret
In appreciation for their being and doing

Contents

Acknowledgments

Although several hundred people were involved with this system in its development, three people have been almost as close to the writing of this book as I have.

John James, my very competent colleague and beloved son, has been closely involved with the development of the original theory and procedures for personal growth. In fact, he created many of the exercises. Together we refined it by teaching numerous seminars and workshops—to professionals in the mental health fields, and to others who wanted to change their lives in important ways while increasing their self-esteem and happiness.

John's continued commitment to excellence, his deep caring for people and the joy and creativity that are so much part of him, have all been major contributions to my life and work. I am delighted that he is currently writing a leader's guide, which will include exercises useful to psychotherapists, counselors, teachers, and others who work with groups.

Betty Fielding has been much involved in the development of this book and has always given me useful and loving feedback. As a professional, she tested the early versions of the manuscript in courses designed for that purpose. As a friend, she commiserated with me when I was frustrated sometimes by my inability to write the way I want to write. As both friend and professional, she helped for endless hours in the preparation of the manuscript.

Margaret Franklin is the person whose involvement in self-reparenting encouraged me to write this book. I had decided not to write any more. Then her insightful observations and provocative questions stimulated me to write a book on how to achieve happiness. Margaret is currently doing research for her Ph.D. on the use and application of self-reparenting as a psychotherapeutic tool. Her dedication to accurate testing and to personal growth is worthy of great respect, and her lovable and loving ways encourage others to respond in like manner.

I am also grateful to Karen Edwards for help in developing the title. I believe book titles are important, so for several months I had been talking with friends about my struggle to find the right title. Many offered suggestions. Finally the "right" title came while I was driving through Mexico in a VW van with Mary Goulding (with whom I had just led a workshop), my husband Ernie Brawley, Bette and Bill Kreger, and Karen Edwards. We were discussing the creative process and brainstorming potential titles. Karen used the words "It's never too late to be a child." Of course, that's really true. Each of us knew it and was experiencing it there. Only two hours earlier we had all been snorkeling in unbelievably clear water with fantastically beautiful fish! Those words of Karen led to the final title, which I like very much. If it also attracts you, I'm glad. I want people to discover it's never too late to be happy.

As I write these acknowledgments very early in the morning with the sun just coming up, I am thinking of those who will guide others in this process, and those who already do so: especially Roberto Shin-yashiki, M.D., of Sao Paulo, Brazil; Gloria Noriega, M.A., and Emilio Said, M.D., of Mexico City, Mexico; Maria Theresa Romanini, M.D., of Rome, Italy; and Michiko Fukazawa, M.S.W., of Tokyo, Japan, who translated *Breaking Free,* my previous book on the subject. I thank them for their interest.

I am also indebted to many people in several professional organizations. One that has been very important to me since its beginning is the International Transactional Analysis Association (ITAA). Head-quartered in San Francisco, it responds to the professional interests of colleagues throughout the world. Another is the Addison-Wesley Publishing Company which encouraged me to write many of my books including this one. In both organizations the intellectual stim-ulation and genuine affection continually add to my happiness.

In addition to these special persons and organizations, I wish to thank the many who have attended my workshops, listened to my lectures, and come to me for psychotherapy and training. In countries where I have had to lecture in English and rely on translators, your patience and enthusiasm astounded me.

I feel touched by those of you who have written to me from around the world to share your hurts and fears and hopes and achievements. Your letters have been a major impetus to further research, and have stimulated me while developing new theories and techniques. Fur-thermore, your confidence has affirmed me, and reaffirmed what you and I know. It's never too late to be happy!

"SINGIN' IN THE RAIN"
ONE WAY
ONE WAY
DO NOT ENTER
ENTER
TOW ZONE
NO
PARKING
LOADING
ZONE

1 An Action Plan for Happiness

Do you ever ask yourself questions about how to feel happier or how to feel happy more often?

Do you ever feel depressed because you can't seem to hold on to happiness you had felt in the past?

Do you ever wonder about your chances of being really happy in the future?

If so, this book is for you. It is an action plan to increase your chances for happiness, even if you thought you'd given up on being happy. Lots of things interfere with a person's being happy—a bad marriage, an unpleasant job, difficult relationships, not enough money, a sad experience, being treated unfairly. But even if life hasn't always seemed fair to you, you *do* have another chance at happiness, and only you can make it happen. *It's never too late to be happy!*

In a career exploration workshop where people were discussing possible job changes, one woman said, "It doesn't matter too much what kind of work I will do because I am going to make a career out of being happy."

In life, many things seem to occur by chance. Other things occur by design. This book gives you a design for happiness. The design is a plan that really can work—if you want it to work and are willing to try it out.

In order to prepare yourself for this action plan, think for a moment. If you were writing a dictionary how would you define happiness? How do you feel, talk and act when you are happy? At what times in your life did you deeply experience this wonderful feeling?

Everyone hopes for happiness, but for many, it seems to be beyond reach. It doesn't have to be that way. If you were to wake up in the morning and think "I'm going to be happy today," what would that mean to you? Would it mean that at some time during the routine of the day you would experience happiness? Does it mean you expect happiness only if you were to achieve or acquire something? Is it possible that both can be true?

Happiness sometimes comes as a surprise—for example, when you receive an unexpected gift. It can come with less surprise but equal pleasure if you perform successfully after long, intensive practice. Moments of elation can occur when you have a creative idea, a visit from a dear friend, or a paycheck that enables you to pay all the bills. Happiness occurs when your body is running well, when the weather looks and feels the way you want it to, when your dog welcomes you eagerly or your cat purrs in your lap, when the flowers you planted bloom, when the meal you prepared turns out just right, and when the people you are with are interesting and enjoyable. We've all known similar moments, and we know we want more of them. How can we become more aware of the innumerable possibilities for happiness?

Although happiness is usually associated with *feeling* good, an understanding of how we interpret it for ourselves is useful. Some people only achieve happiness when they finish a task, while others are happy with what precedes the finish. For example, when making love, some people are happiest at the climax while others are happier during the process that leads up to it. As another example, in competitive sports happiness is more likely to be felt at the moment of winning, while in non-competitive sports, like hiking or river rafting, happiness is more likely to lie in the process; arriving at the chosen destination is important, yet it seldom tops the excitement of getting there. In this book we will look at the process or pursuit of happiness as well as the final goal. Here you will find achieving happiness to include teaching yourself, encouraging yourself, and building your self-esteem. You will learn that true happiness isn't something dependent on events in your life. True happiness grows out of adjusting your outlook—so that the good things in your life take precedence over the bad.

To pursue happiness often requires a basic re-decision about your *right* to be happy. Children make decisions about whether they are entitled to love and happiness, though they may not be aware of having done so. If you find that your childhood decisions are not realistic or conducive to growth, you can re-decide.

We all need someone who encourages healthy re-decisions and reinforces them with positive statements (affirmations). An *affirmation* is a firmly declared opinion that reveals an underlying positive value: "You are important just because you are alive" or "You are really lovable and loving" or "You are capable of great achievements." As they grow and develop, children hear many affirmations. The most common affirmations are for being alive, for having the sexual identity they have, and for achieving certain things parents and teachers consider important. Usually affirmations are verbal; occasionally they are nonverbal in the form of a smile or a pat on the back.

The effects of childhood are with us long after we become adults but, as we'll see, we have the ability to re-evaluate them and take control of our actions. To move from discontentment to happiness, we need to convince ourselves that it is our right to be happy and to pursue happiness with energy and commitment. It's important to believe it's never too late to be happy and the pursuit of happiness is a human right.

Experiencing happiness and actively pursuing it give an added dimension to life. Happiness generates more changes for liberty and most people would agree that life, liberty and the pursuit of happiness have enormous value. Therefore, this book is about how to liberate yourself from some of the effects of negative experiences. Then you can live life more fully with greater chances of success in finding the happiness you've always wanted.

Understanding the Beginning

You were born as the result of two persons coming together. These two persons, your natural parents, may or may not have wanted you, may or may not have been physically and emotionally healthy, may or may not have had the skills and resources to care for you adequately. Whatever the situation, you probably have wished from time to time that your parents had given you something more.

The "something more" could have been more tenderness, more sympathy for your hurts, more protection from ridicule, more encouragement for your academic achievements, more appreciation for you as a person, or more freedom to be you.

You may have wished that your parents had shown you how to do more things, or that they had listened to your ideas and accepted your feelings when you expressed them. Whatever your age now, you may still feel angry if your parents were preoccupied with their own interests and didn't treat you as if you were important. You may still feel deeply sad if your parents died or deserted you. You may have wondered from time to time what you would be like now if your parents had been different.

Perhaps your parents constantly urged you to be on time, to hurry. "Don't be late!" can be a useful message if children are dawdling in the morning before school. But too much rushing gives a child another message: "Don't take time to enjoy!" Children (and adults) occasionally need the kind of enjoyment that comes from watching a flower open to the sun, even when there are tasks to be accomplished.

When they are constantly pressured, children may grow to believe that there is no time to enjoy the beautiful moments of living: when happiness flashes with its myriad of colors across the mind's horizon, when the "music of spheres" is heard as a beautiful symphony of sound, when one's body moves in harmony to the dance of life. The child who hurries to avoid being "too late" may grow up to be an adult who feels it is always too late.

But it is not too late. It is not too late to catch happiness as it flies, and to celebrate in the process of doing so.

Most people have experienced the sense of being outside of time. They may be surprised when they look at the clock and note that what felt like seconds was measured in hours, or what seemed like hours was measured in minutes. Regardless of the unhappiness in your past, you can live now, feeling alive and expectant as you take time, or move outside of time, to discover it's never too late to be happy.

This book will show you that whatever you thought and felt about your parents then, whatever you think and feel about them now, you can revise. You can also revise your present and your future life by building a new Parent into your personality, one that will assist you with your search for happiness.

What Is a Personality

There is no firm agreement on the meaning of *personality*. As the word comes from the Latin *persona*, which means "mask," some theorists claim personality is what a person shows to the world while hiding other parts of the self. Other theorists see personality as a complex set of responses that are observable. "You are what you do" is their orientation. They de-emphasize the hidden aspects. Still other theorists view personality from a "self theory" and focus on the internal mechanism that controls behavior. Some believe in "trait theory." Traits are inherited or acquired and tend to be persistent. They are part of the neuropsychic system that determines how stimuli is perceived.

Whatever orientation is taken to the word *personality*, it is generally agreed that personality can be described in terms of *consistent behavior patterns*. However, there is no general agreement on the *origins* of the consistent behavior. The disagreement, sometimes called the "nature versus nurture" or "genes versus environment" controversy, is generations old and continues to be debated. The nature side of this controversy can be recognized in a statement such as "He inherited his temper from his father." This indicates a belief in the "nature," or genetic, origin of certain consistent behavior patterns. Someone taking the opposite point of view, the "nurture," or environmental, position, could make the statement "What can you expect of a person from that background!" This indicates a belief that family patterns—indeed, the total culture—is what determines personality.

Most theorists today believe both views are true. The effects of inherited genes on personality are real. So, too, are the effects of many cultural determinants. Yet each theorist is likely to stress one position more than the other.

This author's orientation is one that recognizes the impact of inherited traits, yet focuses more directly on the many cultural determinants, including the backgrounds of our parents, the development of our unique family systems, and the effects of teachers, peers, and other significant persons who sometimes function as our substitute parents.

Exercise: My Personality

The study of personality is fascinating. The study of your own personality can be even more stimulating. To begin such a study, sit back, take a couple of deep breaths, and relax for a moment. Let your memory drift back to when you were a child. See yourself as you once were. Try to hear your words and the tone of your voice when you speak. Then reflect on the following:

• *What kind of personality did you have?*

 Which of your traits do you think you inherited?

 Why do you think that?

• *Which of your personality traits do you think you developed in response to your total environment?*

 Why do you think that?

• *Now describe your personality as it seems to be in your current life.*

 How is it similar to the way you were in childhood?

 How is it different?

• *Now reflect on how other people might have described your personality when you were a child and how they might describe you now.*

The Personality Theory of Transactional Analysis

Many psychological systems do not have a personality theory. Personality is assumed, but the structure of it—the *whys* of its development, and the *hows* of changing the structure—are widely ignored. Transactional analysis has a specific personality theory. This theory maintains that there are three major parts to everyone's personality. These are called the Parent ego state, the Adult ego state and the Child ego state. (Capitalized, these words will refer to personality; not capitalized, they will refer to people.)

When people are in the Parent ego state, they are likely to have opinions similar to those their parent figures once had, and to act in similar ways. They may be critical of people who are different, or nurturing with people who need help.

When people are in the Adult ego state, they are processing material in the here and now. They observe, compute, analyze, and make decisions on the basis of facts, not fancy. Being grown up is not the same as being in the Adult ego state. Many grown-ups act like children or parental dictators.

When people are in the Child ego state, they feel and act as they did when they were young—with curiosity and enthusiasm, sadness and withdrawal, anger and rebellion, compliance and hopelessness, and so forth. The younger they are, the freer they are to act spontaneously and express their feelings openly. Then, as they grow up, they often give up the freedom to express themselves naturally and struggle to modify those qualities that are disliked by parent figures.

The TA diagram of personality is represented by three stacked circles: the Parent at the top, the Child at the bottom, and the Adult between the two, often serving as a referee. For example, each ego state may have a different belief system about the value of freedom and happiness, and the clear-thinking Adult may need to referee between the Parent and the Child to decide what is practical and possible.

Refereeing is frequently necessary, because the Parent ego state is often turned on, knowingly or unknowingly. Then the old slogans, injunctions, permissions, and admonitions are replayed like a videotape. When the Parent tape is on, it is heard by the inner Child, who may comply, rebel, procrastinate or try to ignore the internal messages.

Much of the dialogue that goes on inside people's heads is about expectations between the Parent and Child. At one time in everyone's personal history their parent figures were real people who could be seen, heard, and touched. Then the parents became incorporated into the Parent ego state. So, too, the Child was once a real little boy or girl who became covered by the body of a grown-up. Though covered and hidden, the Child remains active, especially when hearing *internal* parent messages (as she or he once heard), or *external* parent messages. External parent messages often come from others on the job or in the home, and a person's responses to them are often the same as they were in childhood. When the Parent part of the personality is restructured, a person can experience a sense of liberation and feel free to be happy.

Imagining a New Life

Relax for just a moment and imagine how life would be if you were freed from some negative self-images and consequently had more self-esteem. Imagine having high energy to put into things that are important to you and that could increase your happiness. Imagine what the world could be like if people were committed to helping each other become liberated and committed to encouraging each other to be happy.

All people have the capacity to imagine. We are born with it. Because of this we can visualize an environment where we are free to grow and change. Visualization has been proven to be a potent tool in physical and emotional change. Negative visualization often leads to negative results. Visualizing oneself to be healthy and happy motivates a person to pursue health and happiness. This book will help you make real what you have imagined. It is an action plan. As you free yourself from some of the negative self-images you carry from the past, you will experience happiness more often and for longer periods of time than you thought possible. At the core of your being, you will know the increasing strength that comes when you direct your energies to making your hope of happiness a reality.

Parenting and Reparenting

Many people feel unhappy or inadequate because as children they did not receive enough positive affirmations, and they do not now feel entitled to give them to themselves. They put a low value on their own rights to life and liberty and happiness. They need a new inner Parent to encourage them.

Parenting is what actual parents, step-parents, foster parents or grandparents do and say to children as they are growing up. Generally they take care of them, teach them, guide them, and even play with them. Parents may do it well, fail dismally, or be just so-so—partly competent and partly incompetent for the task.

Some parents, even after their children become adults, continue to treat them as though they were still very young and, directly or indirectly, tell them what to do and how to do it. These parents don't want to give up their advice-giving roles and may try to restrict their grown children in many ways. In response to these controlling parents, some people remain obedient and relinquish their chances to experience freedom and happiness. Feeling inadequate to take charge of their own lives, they comply with the controls and restrictions applied to them by others. Other people, instead of complying with parents, rebel against them directly or by procrastination or simply try to avoid them.

Reparenting is different from parenting. It is usually done by persons who are not the actual parents. They are substitute parents who give different messages that the original parents once gave.

Reparenting is not a new phenomenon. Since the beginning of time, persons have acted as substitute parents to others—with or without awareness of it. Women have done this more frequently than men, yet men have also assumed parenting functions. Both fiction and nonfiction, ancient and contemporary history, are full of examples of grandparents, aunts, uncles, older siblings, even friends, who acted as substitute parents. Even an institution may have this role, and shape the development of a child in positive or negative ways.

The most common substitute parents are teachers, and healthy children tend to seek out teachers who support their independence and growth and avoid those who interfere with it. A teacher who says "You're very intelligent" may effectively reparent a child who originally was programmed with "You're stupid."

In many cases the values and lifestyles of these substitute parents are so influential that they are incorporated into the personalities of their charges without awareness. If teachers' values are those of the earlier parents, a person's personality may be damaged. If they are better, there are likely to be positive results. However, reparenting by others may not necessarily lead to a sense of independence and feelings of happiness. It is in *self*-reparenting that these positive values are more likely to occur.

Exercise: Affirmations for Being and Doing

Let yourself remember what it was like when you were growing up. What kind of affirmations were you given? By whom? Were the affirmations for being the person you are or for doing particular things?

Affirmations for Being	From Whom	Affirmations for Doing	From Whom

Consider the above patterns. Do you need new affirmations for being or doing?

If so, what might they be?

Do you need affirmations so you are freer to pursue happiness? If so, what might they be?

Exercise: Important People

List some of the important people in your current life. Consider how they parent you. Do they give advice, do things for you, or tell you how you should change? What else?

Important People to Me	How They Parent Me	How It Affects Me

• *Do you need more parenting people in your life? If so, why and how?*

• *Do you need fewer parenting people in your life? If so, why and how?*

• *What "more" or "less" do you need from other people that you could also develop in your new inner Parent?*

Self-Reparenting for a New Life

Self-reparenting is different from reparenting. Self-reparenting is a new theory with very specific procedures based on a personal decision to become a new Parent to oneself.

Self-reparenting is a theory and a procedure for changing the Parent ego state. The word *self* indicates that *you will decide for yourself* what additions are needed in your Parent that will then allow you to find happiness in the world around you ... and in yourself.

In self-reparenting you will not discard the historical parent figures that are now in the Parent part of your personality. Instead, you will add a new Parent, who will have qualities your own parents did not have. The qualities of your new Parent will be the ones you decide to develop in order to enhance your life and the lives of others. Notice how the accompanying diagram illustrates this.

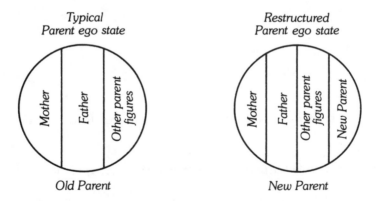

Some things in your old Parent were okay. Other things were not. When self-reparented, your new Parent will compensate, defusing negative qualities that might interfere with your continuing growth and happiness and supplementing your strengths. As you self-reparent, you will learn how to be more effective in taking charge of your life and change what you decide you want to change.

Self-Reparenting for Happiness

The decision to change your life and accept happiness is not an easy one to make. It is often the result of a crisis, sometimes the result of day-after-day unhappiness and desperation. In either case, a person may become physically ill, emotionally distraught, or deeply despairing, and claim "I can't stand myself any more, I wish I were dead," or "I just can't go on this way day after day" or "All things considered, I ought to feel like a success, but instead I feel like a failure. There ought to be more to life than this."

Thus dissatisfaction, unhappiness, physical or emotional pain often create the motivation to change. Some people deny their unhappy feelings. They pretend to others and to themselves that they don't have them.

One way to discover whether or not you would feel better by learning how to be a good parent to yourself is to ask yourself these questions.

• How would I be different if I'd had ideal parents when I was little?

• What would those ideal parents be like?

Answering these two questions reveals the challenge of self-reparenting. You are setting out to restructure part of your personality by adding a new Parent, one that you design for yourself to fit your unique needs. This new Parent will encourage you in your "being" as well as your "doing," will encourage you in playing as well as working, will encourage you in recognizing your lovability as well as your capacity to love. With this kind of internal Parent, you will be freed to go out in pursuit of happiness!

When you are engaged in self-reparenting, you may choose to use others as guides, teachers or therapists. However, only you can determine what needs to be restructured in your Parent. You do this with the awareness that there are many possible choices. The choices you make will be based on what it will take to overcome the obstacles in your way, and allow you to be happy. As each person is unique, each person has unique needs for a new Parent. For example, persons who have had very critical parents and who have become workaholics may decide that they need something more, a new parent that allows them to take time out for relaxation and enjoyment.

People who had overprotective parents may have difficulty taking risks. They may continually expect others to take care of them and make their decisions. They need a new inner Parent who will encourage them to be independent and assertive. When this is accomplished, such people feel much stronger and will experience the new Parent as someone inside who is "on their side."

When the motivation to change is present, self-reparenting can begin. There are eight basic steps.

First comes the awareness that personal change is needed, that something important in life seems to be missing within. The "something missing" is a nurturing parent who respects feelings and encourages clear thinking, freedom, autonomy, and joy.

Second is a reflection on parents in general, common parenting styles, and common responses to them.

Third comes the analysis of your own parent figures who, for better or worse, are incorporated into your personality structure.

Fourth is discovering what your inner Child needs and wants, and how to start getting it.

Fifth is deciding what is possible to get and who could assist in the process.

Sixth is clarifying the various sources of personal power that you are able to mobilize, so that you can take care of many of your needs and wants.

Seventh is the process of learning how to make contracts with yourself that will enhance your life.

Eighth is celebration—to emphasize your newfound courage to be and do. With these eight steps, you'll have a new, loving Parent within who will treat you with dignity, respect, and care, and see that you get the same treatment from others. You'll have new hope, new successes, new happiness. You'll be on your way.

Getting Started

Each of the exercises in this book is designed to assist you in your self-reparenting. For maximum effectiveness, take a few moments and do them as they emerge in the text . None of the exercises will be "too much work," although some may entice you to reflect at deeper levels about who you are, how you got to be that way, and what you want your life to be in the future. You'll be working on *you* and, like a detective or research scientist, searching for clues that lead you to a greater understanding of yourself and the many potentials still waiting for you to develop and express them. Like putting together a jigsaw puzzle, suddenly you'll find a brightly colored piece of your life that will fall into place and open your mind to the larger pattern of your life. Start now!

Exercise: Imagining Your Ideal Parent

Get into a comfortable position and imagine you are looking at a good-sized TV screen on which the story of your life is being played. Spend a few moments looking very closely at yourself as you now are, then fill in the following:

If I had had ideal parents when I was little, I would now

The ideal parents would have been

They would have acted

I could begin now to be an ideal parent to myself by

I think I will begin now because if I do, I will experience a greater sense of liberation, and that will help me in my pursuit of happiness.

_____   _____
     Date   Signature

Sept 8/85   Katherine Q̶

- be contented to be me .
  have a since of self worth
  no how to make decisions
  + set goals .

- ~~supportive~~ realized I was
  a person not a possession,
  taught me dicipline, helped
  me set goals + realize them
  let me know I was an
  individual with needs separate
  from everyone else + them.
  they would have celebrated
  with me when I did well not
  just when it was something
  that helped them .

- interested , serious
  supportive

- I liking + respecting myself
  listening to my needs.
  setting goals large + small
  + celebrating when I achieve

Happiness is freedom to enjoy

Affirmation for being is the basic foundation

2 Expanding Your Options

As a child, did you ever run away from home (or want to run away) because your parents didn't understand you?

Do you ever wonder how life would be now if you had had different parents?

Did you ever compare your parents with someone else's and feel ashamed, or proud?

Do you still feel as if you were tied to your parents and not yet liberated?

If so, you need to restructure the parent part of your personality so that you can get on with life and the happiness it has to offer. The first step of this self-reparenting process is to become aware that when you were little you did not get everything you needed. In this chapter you will discover what some of those things were, and expand your options. You will also learn about typical parenting styles, positive and negative. You will analyze responses to these styles and consider their long-term effects.

Longing for Something More

Most people, no matter how much they have or how happy they seem, yearn for something better. This longing is natural. The "more" may be more security, more self-esteem, or more freedom. In general, the "more" is wanting more out of life.

Some people have adequate, even superior, parenting. Yet they too want something more—more opportunities for growth and self-actualization, for travel, for excitement, for a better job, or for happier home life. Like people who had poor parenting, they also want more security, more self-esteem, and more freedom. What is defined as "more" to one person may mean "nothing" to another. This depends upon the values each holds and how each of them defines success.

Wanting more is not uncommon

Exercise: More for Me

Consider what you wanted more of at various ages: More peace in the family instead of conflict? More security? More attention? What?

During preschool years I wanted more

During early school years I wanted more

During high school I wanted more

During young adult years I wanted more

Since then I have wanted more

• *Is there a pattern in what you have wanted more of?*

• *If you had had it, how would your life be different?*

• *What do you want more of now?*

• *How would it affect your life if you got it?*

• *How would you feel?*

• *What would you say to yourself?*

More Satisfaction

When people want more of something, or more of someone, it is because they believe it will bring them happiness, or at least a higher level of satisfaction. Satisfaction is experienced as quiet pleasure, relief, peace, well-being, or calmness. Needs or desires are gratified, at least for the moment, and the mind, body, and emotions feel in balance.

A balanced state automatically reduces the body's response to stress. This is why many people learn to comply with authority figures when they are children. The stress of rebelliousness often takes too great a toll. When needs and desires are constantly thwarted—either by parents or by internal mechanisms of denial or despair—the awareness and longing for something more may be lost. It can be rediscovered. When that occurs, a person is likely to feel dissatisfied. This has positive value. Dissatisfaction often is a motivating force in this pursuit of happiness!

Enjoying work brings satisfaction

Exercise: A Satisfying Life

There are several ways to think about the various areas of life. The pie chart shows one of them.

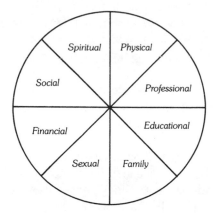

• *If you are very satisfied, put a double plus (+ +) in that segment.*

• *If somewhat satisfied, put a single plus (+) in that segment.*

• *If somewhat dissatisfied, put a single minus (−) in that segment.*

• *If very dissatisfied, put a double minus (− −) in that segment.*

The double minus will need the most radical change, and a strong you to reparent that area in your life. The single minus will also need change, yet it may be less difficult to effect.

The single plus will simply need positive reinforcement, so that you maintain and solidify your successes in this area. The double plus is like an unlimited savings account that you can keep drawing on, yet the principal keeps growing.

The pluses reflect strengths that you have and can use to advance the cause of happiness in your life.

More Success

Success, or "more success," is interpreted differently by different people. Success to one person could be a new job. To another it could be good grades in school or getting a new car. Success could also be improved health or appearance, improved family life or friendships. It could be winning a race, flying a kite, gathering a bouquet of flowers, preparing a gourmet meal, singing a song, dancing a dance.

Success takes many forms. Whatever form it takes, people who experience success feel a sense of achievement and, for the moment at least, some measure of happiness.

Some people feel most successful when they have to work hard to overcome major obstacles, like learning to control a drinking habit or to walk after a bad accident. Other people view success as coping with specific daily tasks. To these people getting out of bed, leaving the house and going to work is success for the day. Coping reasonably well on a daily basis with a physically or emotionally ill family member may be seen as success. Still other people view success as the achievement of long-range goals such as graduation from college, learning to play the piano, being voted into public office, securing a job promotion, or improving a relationship that is falling apart.

When people hold one view strongly, and value one kind of goal (short-term, long-term, difficult to achieve) while discounting others, they miss out on happiness. Moments of success may seem hollow, and they may feel trapped by circumstances beyond their control or by what they consider their personal failures.

The longing for something more is most fully satisfied in people who see value in achieving daily tasks, value in achieving long-range goals, and value in finding the courage to solve crisis situations.

Exercise: Owning Your Successes

*Many people easily recall their failures but forget their successes.
They may ignore successes like graduating from school, managing a
difficult job, or coping with a critical illness. They may not
compliment themselves for breaking a bad habit or learning how to
use money and time responsibly. They may "forget" how they
overcame fear of people by going to a class or joining a club or
singing in a choir. Thinking of themselves as failures, they deny their
successes. This exercise is so you will "own up" and accept your
successes as valid.*

Successes in daily tasks and short-term goals	*Successes with long-term goals*	*Successes in overcoming major obstacles*

To what do you attribute your success?

Exercise: Models of Success

Recall several successful people you have known personally or through the media, and evaluate what they did to achieve success. For example, were they very persistent? Did they establish realistic goals? Dare something new? Ask for help if necessary? What?

Successful persons	*In what ways were they successful?*

What criteria did you use to decide these persons were successful?

How do your criteria reflect your own view of success?

Exercise: Success and Failure in Childhood

Get into a comfortable position. Let your memory drift back to childhood situations when you experienced success or failure. How old were you? How did you feel? What did you think?

How did your parents and other parent figures respond? Were they critical, applauding, or indifferent?

My age	Situation	Successes	Parents' responses to me

Now recall some of your failures and how your parents responded.

My age	Situation	Failures	Parents' responses

• *As you review some of your childhood successes and failures, does a pattern emerge?*

Were your successes generally in academics?

In sports?

In friendships?

In hobbies?

Something else?

Were your failures in a specific field?

• *Are there any clues to what you need when you design a new inner Parent?*

More or Less at Home

The first sense of self as a success or failure develops within the home, regardless of what the home is like. Some homes are like prisons, some are like sanctuaries. Some are like playgrounds or circuses or hospitals or hotels or schools.

One person might say, "I feel like myself when I'm at home." Someone with the opposite view might retort, "It's only when I'm away from home that I feel like myself."

"Home" is a joyful word if you like your home and the people in it. If not, the word *home* may elicit negative feelings such as anger, despair, and dread.

The most common reason people are unhappy at home is that, when they were little, their home was not a happy place to be. Home may have been depressing, or a place of unduly hard work or punishment. The parenting they received there was not conducive to a future successful home life.

All homes have an emotional environment; it may be cold or warm, hostile or loving. The people who live there create the climate, and the climate in turn affects the people. More important than size, location, or furniture are the persons, who have the power to create a heaven or a hell for themselves and the others.

Some people like their homes, some detest their homes, and still others feel deeply ambivalent. Those who are negative usually believe something was missing in their homes when they were young and conclude that, as a consequence, something is missing inside of them. The missing part is awareness of their own lovability and their right to be respected. Some struggle for years to fill this void, then give up in despair. Others recognize the problem and decide to design a better home for themselves, one that contributes to success, not failure. Self-reparenting accelerates this process.

Awareness of what went wrong at home during childhood ("Don't you dare make any noise or I'll whip you so hard you won't forget it") can motivate some people to create a warm and loving home— very different from what they endured. Dissatisfaction with a current home environment can also motivate people to change. They may move to get more sunlight, hang a favorite picture on the wall, throw away the junk they saved, or invite friends in.

Each person has a dream of what home should be like. The dream may be of a sophisticated or convenient apartment; a simple cabin with a scenic view of majestic mountains; a farm with many acres of waving wheat or livestock; a house in the suburbs with a picket fence and roses. Even a castle by a river may be part of a dream.

The old saying "A man's home is his castle" implies the freedom to live as one chooses. It is a way of saying that people should be in charge of their own lives at home, if nowhere else. It implies that people have the right to rule their private lives, and this rule cannot be breached without loss of happiness.

The issue of who does or should rule a household is often debated. When two or more people vie for dominance, friction erupts. Competitiveness replaces cooperation. Power plays become common. Children may compete for a parent's attention and vice versa. Parents may compete with each other. They may argue, shout, rant, and rave to try to prove their superiority over the others.

In a home environment, where cooperation usually leads to happiness, competition usually leads to pain. The words "Be it ever so humble, there's no place like home" may be only fantasy. In self-reparenting, the longing for something more can create a new reality. People can learn to enjoy their homes, and they can learn to enjoy being at home in the world.

Exercise: No Place Like Home

Put yourself in a comfortable position. Relax any tension you may experience in your body. Then turn on an imaginary TV set and switch the dials until pictures of the places you lived when you were young begin to form on the screen in front of you.

Look carefully at yourself in each of your "homes" and observe how your sense of self is forming your feelings of success or failure.

• *What word (such as prison or sanctuary) would you use to describe each home?*

• *Who does the ruling? Are people satisfied with the rule? Does the rule change hands? If so, why, and what happens next?*

• *Is there a crown prince or princess? Slaves or servants? Who plays these roles?*

• *Do children rule at times (perhaps when the rulers are away)? What is their ruling style?*

Life, Liberty and the Pursuit of Happiness

For most young children, their parents rule the world, lay down the law, and decide which gifts to give and which to withhold. Children are particularly alert to the gifts of liberty, given or not given. Like soldiers on leave, they believe liberty leads to happiness. "Wow, I don't have to do any homework tonight!" "They said I could watch any TV program I want!" "Guess what! Mom said I didn't have to clean my room this week." "Dad's letting me stay out hours later than he used to."

Of course liberty, when given by others, does not always lead to happiness. Not doing homework may lead to misery at school. Watching TV may lead to boredom or nightmares. Living in dirt or confusion may contribute to feelings of shame or inadequacy. Staying out late may interfere with health and success.

On the other hand, liberty given by others may feel like paradise. People liberated from a concentration camp or a penal institution know this feeling, as do those liberated from the fear of a life-threatening illness or operation. "You're going to be fine" from a respected physician leads first to relief and then to elation; there is an attitudinal turning back to life and the pursuit of happiness.

Going beyond this, it is the sense of *internal* liberty that enhances life at an even deeper level. When liberation is internally generated, by internal support systems, life is experienced as full, rich, and often happy. Self-reparenting contributes to this development.

Exercise: If I Ruled the World

People who are liberated, and who know some happiness in their own lives, often imagine what they would change if they ruled the world. Their fantasies often involve helping others.

People who are neither liberated nor happy also imagine what they would do if they ruled the world. Often their fantasies are about hurting others, to get even for having been hurt themselves.

How about you?

When I am unhappy some of my ruler fantasies are:

When I am happy some of my ruler fantasies are:

The implications for developing my new Parent are:

Parenting Styles and Child Responses

The rationale for developing a new Parent and learning to be a good parent to yourself is based on the belief that liberation is possible and the pursuit of happiness is a human right. It is also based on the experience that a new internal Parent can counteract the negative parts of the old one and that life can, at least sometimes, be beautiful.

In brief, typical parenting styles that interfere with children's growth toward autonomy include being overly critical, too protective, inconsistent, argumentative, uninvolved, super-organized, or emotionally needy.

Overly critical parents say such things as "You're stupid and you'll never amount to anything," or "Can't you ever do anything right?" or "Get lost." When in the Parent part of their personality, people who had overly critical parents will use these same words to themselves or others, or embody them in nonverbal behavior.

When in the Child part of their personality, listening to their Parent tapes like a ventriloquist's dummy, they may think or say "I don't get it; I guess I'm getting stupid," "I'm sorry, but I don't understand," or defiantly, "You can't make me."

Overly protective parents say such things as "I'll drive you whenever it rains," "Let me do it for you," "Don't worry, I'll take care of everything," or "Now you just tell me if those kids are mean to you." When in the Parent part of the personality, persons who had overly protective parents will act syrupy toward other grown-ups as well as toward children.

When in their Child, they will act overly dependent, always looking for care and protection or rebelliously refuse any help from others.

Inconsistent parents say one thing one day and something different the next. On a Tuesday such a parent may say "I worry about you. You must come home on time," and on Wednesday, say "I don't care what you do, just leave me alone." When in the Parent part of their personality, persons who have had inconsistent parents will act similarly, vacillating in what they expect from others. They may be seen by others as unfair in their demands.

When in their Child, they will feel unsure and frequently check others out, trying to find out what others are thinking or feeling. They constantly look for nonverbal signs and are not surprised by inconsistency.

Argumentative parents often disagree with each other and other people about many issues. Their arguments may be loud, even vituperous, or quiet, even rational, or bitter, even cruel, or sarcastic, not fun. Arguments may arise over work, education, money, leisure time, sex and sex roles, how to rear children, or just about anything. Each parent may take an opposing view, such as "Work until you drop dead" versus "Don't work; let someone else support you."

People with argumentative parents often have an inner battle within their Parent ego state. They are likely to act toward others first as one parent did, then as the other. They may frequently go around looking for a fight.

When in the Child part of their personality, on the other hand, they may feel frightened by loud voices and tend to withdraw when faced with conflict and feel scared when it occurs.

Uninvolved parents may stay away from home a lot. Or, when at home, they don't listen, don't share their feelings and ideas. They may isolate themselves in a particular room or activity and say "Don't bother me, I'm busy." They may act like the proverbial absentminded professor, forgetting birthdays and other special occasions. When relating to others, people who had uninvolved parents will either act distant, or they will withdraw and be uninvolved, as their parents once were.

When in the Child part of their personality, such people often act friendly but unsure. They may search diligently for someone who will act like an involved parent, but at the same time doubt that it could ever happen.

Superorganized parents process data continually; they rarely show childlike warmth and impulsiveness, nor are they either critical or nurturing. People with super-organized parents, when they are in their Parent ego state, are well-organized themselves and expect others to be too.

When in the Child part of their personality, they usually exhibit a pattern of rebellion, indifference, or compliance toward organizations in general and toward organized people in particular.

Emotionally needy parents continually expect to be babied and taken care of, or expect to be cheered up and made happy, or expect to be criticized and forgiven. Such parents often manipulate their children into taking parental roles at home. People who have had emotionally needy parents will express similar emotional needs or repress them.

When in the Child part of their personality, they are more likely to act parental, as they were trained to do in childhood. Such people frequently choose a spouse who acts helpless and needs to be taken care of. They also migrate to jobs in which they will take care of others and ignore themselves.

When remembering your own parents and other parent figures, it is often useful to consider how they tried to control you and how you tried to control them. Some parents control their children with criticism or brutality, some with overprotection or with martyr-like complaints ("You caused me so much pain and grief") or sexual overtures ("If you loved me, you would … "). Other parents control by being perfectly organized and expecting others to be likewise. There are innumerable ways to control or try to control others. Obviously there are also ways to avoid control. Some parents who are disinterested, emotionally disturbed, alcoholic or severely disorganized refuse to set guidelines for the healthy control of children. Children, in response, develop their own patterns of exerting control or trying to avoid it.

Exercise: Typical Negative Parenting

All parents are unique in the details of how they parent. Yet there are some general parenting styles. Your parents and parent substitutes probably acted in both positive and negative ways. This exercise is designed for you to become aware of some of the negatives. Fill in the following columns where appropriate.

Negative parenting styles	Which parent showed this?	How did the style show?	How did you respond?
Overcritical			
Overprotective			
Inconsistent			
Argumentative			
Uninvolved			
Super-organized			
Emotionally needy			

Negative parenting creates unhappiness

Exercise: Typical Positive Parenting

The positive parenting styles listed below are the opposite of those in the previous exercise. For example, the parent who sets reasonable limits is the opposite of the overcritical parent. Or the parent who is able to compromise, negotiate, and make peace is the opposite of the parent who continually argues and fights. What were the positives in your parents? Fill in the columns where appropriate.

Positive parenting styles	Which parent showed this?	How did it show?	How did you respond?
Reasonable Encouraging Consistent Peace-making Caring Relaxed Responsible			

Positive parenting involves fun

Something More or Less?

As you think about the last two exercises, you may observe that you had too much negative parenting or plenty of positive parenting. Or you may have had positive parenting in parts of your life and not in others. As a result, you may feel that something important was missing or that something was out of balance. In either case, you probably wish for something more: someone who would encourage you to succeed more fully. This would be like an ideal new Parent who is guiding and loving you in your search for happiness. You can develop it as you discover more about the parents of your past and what you need for now and for the future. Take time for more.

3 Your Need For Self-Reparenting

Did you ever decide that you would never be like your parents, no matter what?

Have you ever caught yourself speaking or doing something negative just as they once did?

Did you want to be like one of your parents and not the other, only to discover you had some of the disliked parent's traits?

Have you ever noticed that parents sometimes change? And that sometimes they change for the better? If so, you are ready to look at the Parent part of your personality and begin to change what you want to change.

The first step to self-reparenting was to find out what it was all about and how it could be useful. Second was to increase your awareness that parents and other people who parented you were less than perfect. They had weaknesses and they had strengths. You realized that there is always room for improvement.

This step is to show how historical analysis can be used to clarify these parental strengths and weaknesses that you have probably incorporated into your Parent ego state. That is what this chapter is about. You will also discover here what parental teachings interfere with liberty and the pursuit of happiness.

Change Is a Process

Throughout life our bodies change. In youth the changes lead to increased strength and development. With aging the changes lead to decreased strength and development. To some degree, the health and development of a body is influenced by genetics. It is also influenced by accidents, illnesses, and nutrition. Currently there is a widespread and growing cultural awareness of the influence of exercise. Exercise is used to increase bodily well-being and to restructure parts of the body.

There is less awareness that personality structure and restructuring may involve a similar cycle. Research shows that some personality traits seem to be genetically determined. It is also very clear that personality can be changed by training and traumas and the daily conditioning that people experience in their homes, schools, work-places and neighborhoods.

The structure of personality can also change when people decide for themselves that they want to be different. Instead of being fearful and withdrawn, a person may decide to be courageous and outgoing. Instead of acting like a loser, a person may decide to become a winner. Instead of expressing rage and anger in destructive ways, a person may convert the energy into channels that lead to success. Instead of feeling inadequate or stupid, a person may change this self-image and build a personality that is grounded in high self-esteem.

The process is a little like body building. First you determine the weaknesses, then establish the goal. A plan of action comes next. As the plan is implemented, you continually evaluate results so that necessary adjustments can be made as you go. Evaluation of body building includes testing of muscles. Evaluation of personality change is more subtle and subjective, but a sense of expanded awareness and greater satisfaction often point to positive personality change.

When people experience positive new changes, they get excited and want more. Then the *process* of personal growth becomes as important as the product. All of life is a change process. Self-reparenting, the art of learning how to be a good parent to yourself, facilitates positive change.

Change involves a new perspective

Exercise: Are You in Charge?

People change in many ways. Sometimes changes are forced upon them because of circumstances. Sometimes changes just seem to happen. Sometimes they want change and go about making it happen. List some of the changes you have made in your life and how they occurred.

Changes I made	Forced by circumstances	Change just happened	I planned the change

Knowing you can change and being able to develop clear plans for change is a sign that you are in charge. Perhaps there are changes you would like to make and have not made yet.

Future changes I want	*Waiting until forced by circumstances*	*Waiting for it to just happen*	*Planning now so it will happen*

Family Loyalty

Loyalty to parents or family usually stems from your having internalized their values and expectations without being aware of it. When people break with the values and do the unexpected, they often feel guilty—even when the unexpected takes the form of authentic growth and success!

Of course, many families encourage growth and success. The loyalty of a family's members may be based on happy shared experiences, or successful coping with crisis, or authentic expressions of love. However, many children learn to be loyal to the family because they are coerced. "Don't you dare tell anyone or you won't be able to play for a month." Later the bond of loyalty may become a ball-and-chain, seriously restricting thinking, feeling, and behavior. Because young children are so much under the authority of their parents, they are often unaware that the demands for family loyalty may be unjust. Parents who elicit promises from their children for lifetime care create an unjust family loyalty. Children who promise often feel guilty and angry if they become aware that the demand is unjust. Parents also create an unfair family loyalty if they threaten or otherwise manipulate children not to tell anyone about the parents' failings. Trying to keep family secrets can be an impossible obligation.

Isn't it strange that children of any age usually expect their parents to be loyal to them no matter how they mess up their own lives, and parents seem to have similar expectations. When this kind of obligation becomes too great a burden, the relationship often breaks down, sometimes beyond repair.

Exercise: The Tyranny of the Shoulds

Many people live under what has been called "the tyranny of the shoulds." They think they should do this, should do that. A common should is keeping secrets about parents. People often fantasize that something terrible will happen if they don't.

This exercise will help you get in touch with fantasies that could interfere with your evaluating the pros and cons of your parents. Protect the image of your parents as much as you like, just be aware of what it was like then and the possible effect on you.

The way my parents were in private	Fantasies I had about telling someone	The effect of keeping or not keeping their secrets

The Internalized Parents

Some children are reared by both of their biological parents, some by only one. Some are reared by grandparents or foster parents or step-parents. Some are parented by older siblings or nursemaids. Some grow up in institutions where the staff serves as parents.

In any case, these parenting figures are internalized in childhood and become the Parent part of the personality. This Parent part functions in two ways: externally toward other people, and internally toward oneself (especially toward the inner Child).

Most people have more than one parent figure, and their internalized parents may not agree with each other. The result is confusion. For example, one parent may believe religion is important, another parent may strongly disagree. As a result, their children may become ambivalent or take sides against one of the parents. Another kind of parent that confuses children is the one who gives conflicting messages at the same time, or different messages at different times, like "Come close to me" and "Stay away and don't bother me." Other parents may be critical one moment and overly indulgent the next. This also confuses children, who need stability in their lives. As they grow up, they fluctuate between being self-critical and self-indulgent. And so it goes.

Parents who have internalized a belief in their own superiority may be highly critical of others and feel self-righteous about their own values and lifestyles. One of the most important steps in self-reparenting is to analyze the parents of childhood and discover how they are still functioning, whether you are aware of it or not.

You need to explore both the negative and positive aspects in detail. Some people do not want to look at the positive because they are so angry at some of the things their parents did to them. But when they refuse to look at the positive, they deny themselves an important source of strength. This source of strength can be used productively even though some other attributes of their parents were counter-productive.

Some people act and feel as if they were stuck, and consequently are not happy. They harbor so much resentment against their parents that they refuse to admit their parents had any positive attributes at all. They don't want the facts. "I've made up my mind and I'm not going to change it no matter what!" They refuse to examine possible extenuating circumstances for their parents' negative parenting. Other people don't want to evaluate their parents even if their parents were very good, because they think evaluations are disloyal or disrespectful.

People who have been brutalized, sexually molested, or deserted by their parents often find it difficult to recognize anything positive in them. In such cases, an awareness that some of their own positive intelligence and appearance was directly inherited from their parents' genes helps build new self-esteem (and some appreciation for their parents).

When people discover that there were some positive things about their parents despite what may have been parent pathology, they often experience more self-esteem. "Well, my mother was crazy as anything," claimed one woman, "but she sure was a good cook." "My father didn't know how to get along with people, even himself. But he worked hard to support us," affirmed a man who was analyzing his parents' positive and negative attributes.

Eventually most people come to terms with their imperfect, yet understandable, parents. They let go of much of their resentment and sometimes even forgive their parents. They also let go of the unrealistic belief that if their parents had only been perfect, life now would be perfect. They are in a good position to create a new Parent that will reinforce their growing independence and cheer for them enthusiastically in the pursuit of happiness.

Exercise: Analyzing Your Parent Figures

This is one of the most important steps in the entire self-reparenting process. It will help you make some sense out of your parent figures and their influence on you.

List the major parent figures you had in childhood and their positive and negative attributes. Include your biological parents, stepparents, foster parents and any other people (such as older siblings and grandparents) who had responsibility for you.

Mother's Attributes		Father's Attributes	
+	−	+	−

Other Parent Figures

+	−	+	−	+	−

Make additional plus and minus columns if more people parented you.

Exercise: Owning Your Parents

Many characteristics of the parents and parent figures you once had were incorporated into your personality and became the Parent part of your personality. Which ones do you own up to? Which have you rejected?

Positive characteristics of my parents that I sometimes use.	Situations in which I use them.

Negative characteristics of my parents that I sometimes use.	Situations in which I use them.

Characteristics of my parents that I rejected and do not use.	How and when I made this decision to be different.

Parental Injunctions

All children receive messages or injunctions about their worth from their parents, including foster parents, grandparents, older siblings, and other family members, as well as teachers and people who live in the neighborhood. Any or all of these messages contribute to a child's positive or negative esteem.

A child who receives only positive messages will have much less need for self-reparenting than will those who have the opposite experience. However, even if a child has ideal parents, there are often other significant persons, such as teachers, stepparents, grandparents, or older siblings, who give injunctions that interfere with health and happiness.

Injunctions are commands, directives, or orders. The word is used here to refer to statements or acts by parenting figures that adversely affect a child's sense of being alive and well, capable and competent, free and joyful.

There are a number of basic negative injunctions, according to psychotherapists Mary and Bob Goulding. The first two are against *being* itself: "Don't be" and "Don't be you." Two are about relationships: "Don't be close" and "Don't belong." Next are those concerned with personal growth: "Don't grow up" and "Don't be a child." Others are against physical or emotional wellness: "Don't be well" and "Don't be sane." Two are against achievement: "Don't be important" and "Don't succeed."

Don't Be   This is a lethal injunction. It is a message given verbally or nonverbally by parents who do not want a particular child to exist. This can be for many reasons. The parents may be very young, not married, and not able to cope with the problems involved. Or they may believe they already have enough or too many children and not want "one more mouth to feed" or "one more diaper to change." Other parents may be physically or emotionally ill, almost incapable of coping with life at all. Still other parents may dislike each other intensely and see a child as a burden that might put pressure on them to stay together. Then there are an increasing number who don't want children because it would interfere with their careers. The most common responses to "Don't be" are passivity and depression.

Don't Be You   Although this injunction is not as lethal as "Don't be," it is still a devastating attack on a child's identity. It is most strongly given by parents who wish a child were of the opposite sex. Parents may openly complain, "Oh, if you were only a boy" or "I sure wish you were a girl." The child soon learns that his or her basic sexual identity does not please the parents.

Children who are not supposed to be who they are may be dressed and treated as if they were the opposite sex. Sometimes this causes deep despair or confusion, and liberation from it may require extensive professional help.

Don't Be Close   This negative injunction is often given by parents who see themselves as too busy to listen to, comfort, play with, or teach a child. This injunction is also given nonverbally by parents who abandon their children. A child who is abandoned may decide never to love again, or never to be close to a person of the same sex as the parent who left. A child may make a similar decision if a parent dies. Death feels like abandonment.

Another way this injunction is experienced is when divorce, or continuing conflict, splinters a family. When strong bitterness is expressed between parents, they may compete for the affection of a child and issue the message, "Don't be close to that so-and-so of an ex-spouse; only be close to me."

Don't Belong   Children experience this injunction if they are rejected by parents who wish a particular child were not part of the family—often because of some problem a child has. In such cases, it is not unusual for children to fantasize being adopted. Adopted children may feel the same, or more so.

Some children are taught that they are either better than others or not as good as others; thus they, too, may feel like outsiders. If they are rejected by their peers or by their teachers, they can also experience a "You don't belong" message.

Don't Grow Up   This is the command of parents who want their children to remain under their control. In spite of what they say, they do not want children to grow up to think or act independently. They want obedience and compliance to their opinions, ideas, and demands.

Don't Be a Child   This injunction is just the opposite of "Don't grow up." It is often given by parents who themselves act like children. They reverse the parent-child roles and insist that their children care for them—either physically or psychologically—rather than caring for their children.

"Don't be a child" may also be given by parents who are overly ambitious for their children. Pushing their children to compete and be first, such parents often feel inadequate and use their children as compensation for what they miss in themselves.

The same message often accompanies a "Don't be close" injunction given by parents who are too busy and refuse to listen to what they may label as "kid stuff" or "childish concerns." The same message comes through if they continually refuse to play with their children or imply that play is less important than work.

Don't Be Well   This is another injunction given by parents who need to keep their children dependent. After all, if a child is not well, then a parent's attention is required (which may lead the parent to feel important). In some cases the parent may choose to act like a martyr to get sympathy from others for having an unhealthy child.

Don't Be Sane   An injunction to be crazy may be given by parents who do not want their children to be sane because they might see how crazy their parents are. It is also given with remarks such as "You're impossible; you act so crazy." "Can't you think like a rational human being?"

Don't Succeed   Like parents who want others to remain dependent on them, some parents do not want their children to have more success than they have themselves.

Such parents might give the injunction by continually criticizing less-than-perfect grades so that a child concludes "I'm not perfect; therefore I can't succeed." When grown up, these persons may almost reach goals, then do something at the last minute that undermines their achievements.

Don't Be Important   To be important is to be special and to be recognized as such. Children with a "Don't be" or "Don't be you" injunction also believe they are not important as individuals. Their parents may pay more attention to another child, or a job, or a hobby, and use comments such as "Don't bother me" or "Don't be such a nuisance" or "Don't be a show-off; you're no better than anyone else." They structure their time and interactions in such a way that their children conclude "My needs are not important; therefore I'm not important."

Don't ...   This more generalized injunction is like a spell that seemingly paralyzes the person who receives it. It depends on creating fear. "Don't go out of your backyard or something terrible might happen" or "Don't contradict me or something terrible will happen."

People who receive this injunction are continually fearful of an assertive position, of sticking up for themselves, of making decisions, of doing something new, of thinking, of changing, of taking charge of their own lives. Indeed, of everything.

The caring parent is supportive

Exercise: Discovering Negative Injunctions

As you work to understand the effect of your parents and substitute parents on you, consider the following list of injunctions .

Injunction I received	How it was given and by whom	Effect on my life
Don't be		
Don't be you		
Don't belong		
Don't grow up		
Don't be a child		
Don't be well		
Don't be sane		
Don't succeed		
Don't be important		
Don't ...		

If you received any of the above injunctions—directly or indirectly— you will need to develop an ideal Parent message to counteract the old negative ones.

Start now. What could you record as a new tape that you could play to yourself until it is integrated into your personality?

Escaping from Injunctions

Injunctions can be perceived as realistic or not realistic. When they are believed to be real, a child will decide "That's the way I am" ("I don't belong") or "That's the way I shouldn't be" ("I shouldn't be important"). These beliefs about oneself can be very damaging, and a child may decide "I can't ever change. I'm hopeless." When this is the case, a rescuer may be needed who will help the person escape from the deadening commands.

Sometimes, however, children perceive the injunctions to be unfair, inaccurate, or grossly exaggerated. When this is the case, they may make a healthy decision: "I don't believe what my parents wanted me to believe about myself" and "I can rescue myself if I have to." The capacity to seek out people who are willing to throw out a lifeline when life or liberty are threatened is part of self-reparenting. Another part is learning how to rescue oneself.

Escape to freedom

Exercise: Rescuers You Have Known

For most people, things go wrong from time to time. They may turn
to others to rescue them and, if the rescue is forthcoming, they
develop hope. Consider how it was for you.

Situation when I needed rescue	People who rescued me	Ways they rescued me	Positive effect on my life

Perhaps you needed help and there was no one available, so you
called on your own abilities and courage. How has this affected
you?

Consider your capacity and experience at self-rescuing.

Situation when I rescued myself	What I did	Positive effect on my life

"Cultural" Parents

In many ways, cultures and subcultures act like parents. Cultures may be national, racial or ethnic. Your school, your religion, and your neighborhood are subcultures. There are many more. Each tries to dictate what people are suppose to do or not do. Often mottos or repetitive phrases reinforce cultural beliefs. Compliance or lack of compliance with these rules determine whether a person fits in. The problem of fitting in is often experienced by families who move from one part of a country to another. For example, U.S. citizens moving from the South to the North may define courtesy in terms of Southern manners, and feel like a critical parent or uncomfortable child in the new environment.

Culture shock can be painful or pleasureable, as any traveler knows. Culture shock happens when change is so extreme or rapid that people feel disoriented and out of place. They don't yet fit into the new scene. They may hear a different language spoken, notice different actions expected, come up against different laws. Suddenly, in addition to their own parents and the cultural "parents" they know, sometimes like and usually fell familiar with, they have a new cultural parent to cope with.

The same feelings of shock and stress are often experienced when even minor geographical moves are undertaken. For example, transferring from one school to another can be very traumatic if the school culture is different. So can a move from a rural area to a big city, or vice versa. Also, what may seem like a minor move to parents could be a major move to children.

Being of a particular race, religion, class, or ethnic group in a city where the majority of people are different may also lead to confusion or unhappiness (unless the minority has the power). Being part of a dominant group is usually more comfortable than the opposite. Those of the majority often have more opportunities to pursue life, liberty and personal happiness.

People who immigrate to new countries for a job, citizenship, or permanent residence often experience prejudice. Their previous expectations and lifestyles may not fit in to their new life. Some adjust. Others do not. They may be critical of new ways and experience despair, or try to influence others to accept the values they brought with them. They may be ridiculed, ignored or discriminated against in life-threatening ways. Jobs may be hard to get, language barriers overwhelming, and the new country that was expected to be a liberating home may instead be a confusing, even restricting, one.

In spite of this, the search for happiness goes on. Many continue their old customs and form new subcultures of like-minded people. Others adjust to the new culture either happily or unhappily, depending on many variables and on comparisons made to "the way it was back home." Gradually the culture shock disappears.

Exercise: Roots and Uprooting

Most people feel emotionally rooted in the culture and subculture in which they lived as a child. If they move, they may take the culture with them, or be glad to leave it behind.

Moves I have made	From what	To what	Effect on my life

• *Now for a moment sit still and let your mind quiet itself. Reflect on the positive values of your various roots and uprootings.*

• *Consider what new moves and changes you want to that would increase your happiness.*

• *What kind of ideal new Parent do you need to develop to assist you in continuing change and growth?*

Exercise: Your Interacting Cultural Parents

Describe each of the following cultures, as you have experienced them, in three to five words.

The subcultures may be social, ethnic, geographical, socio-economic, religious, etc. Choose a subculture that had or has the most influence in your life. (Some people find their school subculture is crucial to their self-esteem and understanding.)

How I describe my national culture	How I describe my family culture	How I describe one of my subcultures	Effect on me is

Now analyze their strengths and weaknesses and how they were, or are, in agreement or disagreement, and put a plus or minus after each of the above.

- *What advice would an ideal parent give you about the negatives you received from your culture?*

New Power for Change

As you discover the complexities of the parent figures that you internalized, you may from time to time feel either trapped or freed. Perhaps your parents of your past would encourage you to change; perhaps they would fight change, or undermine your change in some less direct way: "Oh, you don't really want that. You know you don't."

Old Parent messages are powerful. New Parent messages can be more powerful if you construct them carefully. After all, the new ones will be more nearly what you inner Child wants to hear. The new ones will be like a loving-parent-and-happy-child alliance that can overcome the old parental master-parent-and-child-serf combination. Designing new messages that are acceptable and life-enhancing may seem difficult, but you can do it. You can restructure the Parent part of your personality so that you feel hopeful and powerful, and use your hope and power to further liberate yourself for happiness.

4 Learning to Be Happy

Have you ever proclaimed with confidence "I can do it if I work at it."

Have you ever complained "I wish somebody would tell me I'm not stupid," or "I wish I liked myself better than I do?"

Do you listen sometimes to your internal critical Parent and suddenly feel lowered self-esteem or fear?

Most people have little or no education in one of the most important tasks any person undertakes—the task of parenting. Sometimes parenting comes easily because of having had good role models. Often it is very difficult. People tend to assume that good parenting happens naturally. Not so.

To be a good parent to others or to oneself requires both motivation and skills. Some people have neither, some have one but not the other, and some have both motivation and skills. Of course, those who have both are the most effective. They recognize that their task is helping children learn how to love, how to think, how to work, and how to play. To accomplish these tasks, parents must be powerful and protective, and they must give children permission to be happy.

Most people could profit by some education about what it means to be a good parent and about the way good self-parenting could change their lives today. Understanding the positive effects of good parenting is necessary for self-reparenting. With an educational program you design for yourself, you will be clearer on on the potency, permission, and protection that you need in your new Parent. You will also see how habitual ways of acting, thinking, and feeling can interfere with your happiness. Furthermore, you may discover that the new Parent you are creating needs to use tough love sometimes and tender love other times. Both can be effective; both can help you in your process of learning to be happy.

Logical Thinking and Creativity

The capacity to think is an important tool that helps liberate people from unhappiness. Developing a new inner Parent involves both creative and logical thinking. Creative thinking includes fantasizing about what an ideal inner Parent would be and logical thinking involves analyzing old Parent figures and deciding what and how to construct a new inner Parent.

One of the important discoveries made within the past few years is that people use their left brain and their right brain for different kinds of thinking. The right brain produces creative, holistic thinking and the left brain produces logical, analytical thinking.

Some people do not trust the potential of their creative thinking and fantasies and exaggerate the value of being logical. They fail to see that their pride in logical thinking may really be part of a grandiose fantasy they designed to enhance their own self-esteem. The opposite can also be true. Some people only pride themselves on their creative thoughts. They do not see that ignoring their capacities to think logically is likely to lead to a life that is out of balance.

Both kinds of thinking are valuable. When balancing a checkbook, the logical skill of analyzing costs and expenditures is useful. However, a creative form of budgeting might solve fiscal problems or increase potential savings. Some people obviously do this better than others.

Both logical and creative thinking are molded by genetic inheritance, childhood conditioning, adult experience, and education. For example, it is generally agreed that intelligence is partly genetic. It has also been proven that intelligence can be raised or lowered during a life span, depending upon motivation, learned skills, and opportunities for growth and development. With high intelligence, some people may perform almost unbelievable feats of logical thinking, for example in the field of mathematics. Yet research shows there are different kinds of intelligence.

High intelligence in one area may not mean a person is bright in other areas. Someone who has high mathematical intelligence may lack the kind of musical intelligence shown by great musicians. Furthermore, being bright does not mean a person will usually think logically or will develop constructive plans of action. Some very intelligent people are clever crooks! Others ignore the information they do have because it does not agree with their personal bias. Furthermore, logical thinking may be labeled "illogical" if it does not coincide with cultural norms.

Whether thinking is logical or illogical, positive or negative, it may nevertheless be creative. Creativity is expressed when the person puts together objects, facts, ideas, feelings, or behaviors in new ways. Creative thinkers don't agree with the commonly held belief that if certain things haven't been done, they can't be done. They trust themselves to think for themselves and redecide poor decisions made in the past. They certainly don't agree with the belief that parents have the sole right to determine their children's future just because they did so in the past.

Exercise: Midpoint Evaluation

Synectic is a word that refers to the novel joining together of elements that are not readily seen as connected. In developing your new Parent, you are using synectic skills because you are using both logic and creativity. This is approximately a midway point in your self-reparenting and a good place to evaluate your progress.

Summarize how you have used your logical thinking so far in self-reparenting:

Now summarize how you have used your creative thinking so far in self-reparenting:

Put the two together and evaluate how you are doing in your pursuit of happiness:

Field Work on Parenting

One of the most effective ways to develop a new Parent is to do "field work" on actual parenting. You actually go out in the field to observe how things are done and how they can be improved. An internship or apprenticeship, where a person is actually doing work under supervision, could be called field work. Many professions require this as part of their training.

In previous generations, apprenticeship and internship in parenting was common. Large families and relatively stable neighborhoods enabled people to observe parenting and decide whether it was adequate or not. Today families are smaller and many people have less time for parenting because they are juggling priorities. Traditional parent education, intrinsic in most cultures, is disappearing here. Because of this, people who are reparenting themselves may know very little about being a parent. That is where the parenting field work comes in. It begins with planned observation.

Planned observation includes going to places where people are parenting young children and observing what is going on—both positive and negative. Supermarkets or department stores are rich fields for observation. Sometimes the parents are harried and the children look hurried, helpless, and hopeless. Sometimes both look happy. Nursery schools and playgrounds reveal a more structured facet of child-rearing that involves directed play. This kind of observation can be very useful if you want to be a better new Parent to yourself.

Another way to further develop your new Parent is to read books on child development, particularly on developing a child's self-esteem. Throughout the study, ask yourself "What am I learning that is new and positive that I could begin to apply to myself?" What kind of parent education do I need that will enhance my ability to be happy?

The Three Ps

Some people find parenting to be relatively easy, even enjoyable. Some do not. Your parents may have found parenting difficult and frustrating. If so, they probably lacked one or more of the qualities needed to be good parents. Good parents have three basic qualities that people may need to develop in the new Parent they create for themselves. These basics are potency, protection, and permission.

Potency is strength. A potent parent is strong in the face of adversity or tragedy, strong when meeting difficult commitments or long-term goals. Being strong does not mean denying or repressing unhappy feelings that may be present. It means going ahead with life in spite of difficulty or negative experiences.

Sometimes going ahead takes courage because there may be a risk of failure. The potent person recognizes this possibility and strives to minimize the risk. He or she also recognizes personal feelings of ambiguity, confusion, or fear and owns up to having them. Owning up to having feelings is not the same as being owned by the feelings. Potent persons are in charge of their own feelings and behavior and they know it. Potent persons also are aware of their belief systems and free to change them when it seems like a good idea.

In self-reparenting, the positive new Parent needs to be more potent than the original parents. If not, the old negative messages may continue to be replayed, and the inner Child will continue to listen. A strong new Parent will not allow that to happen, or will intervene if it starts to occur. An example of intervention is a parent who turns off the TV if a child is watching an inappropriate program. The potent Parent stops the tape from running or, at least, plays a more positive one that drowns out the noise of the past. When the potent new Parent intervenes to cut off old negative tapes, the Child is protected.

Protection is needed by children in order to feel safe and secure. Without protection they usually become fearful grown-ups who are afraid to risk new ventures and afraid to change old patterns of responses. Or they become grown-ups who do not trust others and frequently attack or defend against real or imagined insults.

Protection can be given to the inner Child in many ways. The new Parent, for example, may encourage the learning of martial arts to someone who is afraid of being physically attacked or encourage assertiveness in the face of criticism. Some people who have had indifferent or overly indulgent parents feel insecure and in need of protection because reasonable limits were not established for them as children. Perhaps their parents failed to provide curfews, or allowed them to make too many choices for themselves—whether to stay in school or drop out, whether to go to bed or stay up late, and so forth. The effect on children is that they may feel powerless and lack a sense of direction.

The person developing a new Parent needs to decide on reasonable limits that are protective and contribute to an inner security. A new Parent can insist on proper health care—food, exercise, decent living conditions, and work habits. When people feel protected by potent internal or external Parent figures, they then feel as if they have permission to succeed.

Permission is consent or authorization. It can be given verbally, as in "I think it's great you want to learn something new." A statement such as this encourages a person to learn and be creative. Permission can also be given nonverbally, as with a pat on the back or a warm smile.

People who are frequently depressed, or who feel miserable in some other way, or who are self-punitive or punitive against others, need the permission from an encouraging Parent to break free of this negative cycle. Other people who neither succeed nor fail, live lives of boredom or trivia. They also need permission to turn around and pursue a different road that may lead to happiness.

Exercise: Parenting and the Three Ps

Consider specific areas in your life in which you experienced your parent figures being potent, protecting you, and giving you permission—especially permission to be happy.

When my parents were potent	When my parents were not potent	The effect on me

When my parents gave protection	When my parents did not give protection	The effect on me

When my parents gave permission	When my parents did not give permission	The effect on me

If your parents did not do well in the above areas, what kind of education does your new Parent need to counteract the negative effects? Write it down.

My new Parent needs to

The effect of this on me would be

Teachers as Parents

Teachers often serve as substitute parents and are incorporated into the Parent ego state much as the parents once were. They, too, may give or withhold their potency, protection, and permissions.

By their very position, teachers also teach the basic curriculum for living, and in the process contribute to the personality development of children, often in very positive ways. They show what it is to love by teaching cooperation. They demonstrate what it is to think by teaching problem-solving and research skills. They model what it is to work by teaching how to study and complete assignments. They encourage play by teaching children how to enjoy recess and sports. They assist the shy child to become involved, and the bully to control self instead of trying to control others.

Teachers who inspire the pursuit of happiness may compensate to some extent if a student's home life is miserable. It is not unusual for students to idolize teachers who treat them with respect and encourage their personal as well as intellectual growth.

Sometimes teachers aren't so nice, or they play favorites. Their method of teaching and learning may be too restrictive: "Keep your feet flat on the floor, your eyes on your books, and no talking or you will stay after school!" They may discourage children from socializing or banding together out of their own fear of losing control over their students. Other teachers don't make time for the less-than-perfect students. They don't provide the special motivation or help many children need. Learning can become a dreaded chore. Too much control or not enough help can decrease children's self-esteem. The child may decide, "I'm stupid, I can't think, and I'll never amount to anything."

People who make decisions like "I'm stupid" often become very unhappy. Instead of finding learning easy, or at least interesting, they find the whole process of education more and more difficult. This pattern may continue throughout life so that, even on the job, learning something new is painful.

When we are adults, teachers often come to represent internal authority—the "little voice in the back of our head" who keeps us in line, or makes us do the chores, or finish the assignment, or keep our promises. Sometimes we need this admonishment to do what's best. If our teachers have had a positive influence, the internal teacher will be a gentle reminder. If we had unhappy experiences in school, we may be very hard on ourselves. We need to learn to be good teachers to ourselves.

Teachers' influences on happiness

Exercise: The Three Ps in Problem-Solving

Remember that your teachers were like parents and your parents were teachers. They all taught you a great deal—some good, some bad.

Select a problem you have now that you have not yet solved:

In what ways do you need a potent *parent/teacher to help you?*

What protective *parent/teacher strategies do you need for solving the problem?*

What parent/teacher permissions *would be useful in solving your problem?*

- *Is your life, your liberty, or your pursuit of happiness part of this problem?*

- *Is someone else's life, liberty, or pursuit of happiness part of this problem?*

Keeping in mind that parents are teachers and teachers are parents, get involved with the re-education of your inner Child.

Exercise: Learning the Easy and Hard Ways

People learn in many ways. Sometimes the learning comes the hard way, with struggle, anxiety, or agony. (For example, some people learn out of fear of punishment or after making a costly mistake.) Sometimes learning comes the easy way, without struggle, and with interest and enjoyment.

List five important things you have learned and how you learned them.

Things I learned	How I learned the easy way	How I learned the hard way	The effect on me was

Now sit down and relax your body, especially your facial muscles. Imagine you are in a situation where you need to learn something new and difficult. See yourself there.

• *If you are anxious or confused, see yourself appearing confident and relaxed.*

- *Say to yourself, "I am able to learn many things the easy way." Repeat this several times until you really believe it.*

- *Select something you want to learn now. Say to yourself, "I can learn _____ the easy way."*

A Curriculum for Parenting

Teaching well usually involves knowledge of the subject, interest in helping people learn about it, ability to make the subject come alive and to demonstrate how it can be applied. Any school curriculum consists of various courses that are related to each other in an organized way. Parents need to offer their children a similar opportunity for wholeness. Specifically, they need to teach (often by example) how to love, how to think, how to work, and how to play.

How to love is best taught by providing a home where love is present. Love is more than warm feelings, acts of kindness, nurturing, and approval. Love includes setting limits—saying no as well as yes. Love is sometimes challenged when people are tired, anxious, or critical, or when communication is inadequate and conflict erupts. It is also challenged when tragedy strikes in the form of accident, death, or illness. We need love when despair sets in because a job is lost or a friend betrays us or a colleague doesn't keep promises. Love is not just happiness when things are going well. It includes being present for others when things are not going well.

The need to love oneself is also learned at home. Parents who act like martyrs to their children may believe they are showing love. They are not. They may be over-indulging their children who will, in turn, take a self-centered view of life and over-indulge themselves. Parents who teach love demonstrate by their actions the importance of taking responsibility for yourself and acting in loving ways because you are lovable.

How to think is best taught by encouraging children to do their own thinking and not giving them all the answers. Parents who want their children to think encourage them to observe the external world as well as their internal thoughts and feelings and to think of themselves as unique. They encourage school performance and the use of libraries. They share ideas and assist, if needed, with homework. They treat children like intelligent beings who very often have good ideas and sound solutions to problems.

How to work is best taught by demonstration and involvement. Parents who show their children how to handle tools and machinery, without being critical in the process, help the children develop confidence and self-esteem. Distribution of family chores (dependent upon the ages and capacities of children and the family situation) teaches children that getting the daily work done can enhance life because it leads to order instead of disorder. Like play, work can be over-emphasized. When it is, many people begin to think of it as distasteful. Later they may choose boring jobs that require neither logical nor creative thinking. An effective parent, by example and precept, shows that work is often enjoyable—both the process of doing it and the product when it is done.

How to play is sometimes the most difficult for parents to teach, because they have structured their own lives without play. Thus they demonstrate, in their living and teaching, a "don't enjoy" injunction. Such parents do not know that play is the "work" of childhood. In play, children experiment with life roles. They use their imagination and expand their creativity. Playing with peers, they learn new interpersonal skills and the value of cooperation for achieving goals. So one of the most important parental tasks is encouraging children to play. People whose parents did not value play need a new Parent who does. Laughter often liberates by reducing personal or interpersonal tension. A playful person can laugh and love, think and work, with more enjoyment for life, liberty, and the pursuit of happiness.

Exercise: Basic Education for Living

The basic educational task for parents is helping children learn how to love, think, work, and play. Consider how you learned this in childhood from your parents or parent figures.

Basic education	I learned or didn't learn	I'm satisfied or dissatisfied
How to love		
How to think		
How to work		
How to play		

If you are dissatisfied with what you learned and how you learned it, then you need some re-education.

* *Design one to three short statements for any area of basic education that you missed. Write statements your new Parent could use ("You can learn to think clearly" or "You don't need to be confused".)*

* *Put the statements on 3 × 5 cards and carry them with you. Read them several times a day.*

Education for Feeling

It is impossible in this book to consider all the feelings people have and how these feelings can be dealt with. Yet the new Parent is likely to need some guidance on the subject.

In one way or another, verbally or nonverbally, many children receive parental messages such as "Don't feel" or "Don't let your feelings show." Other children are encouraged to feel some feelings, but not others. They may be conditioned to be scared, yet not allowed to show it, with threats like "If you go on crying, I'll really give you something to cry about." Another way parents educate children about feelings is more subtle. They make statements such as "Big boys don't cry" or "Nice girls don't get angry." These messages need to be updated with statements such as "Boys can cry sometimes, it's natural" and "Girls do get angry sometimes, it's natural." All feelings are natural and need to be respected.

In response to being manipulated by parents, growing children learn to manipulate themselves and their feelings. In choosing of whether to feel angry or sad, they may habitually choose how they felt in childhood. They may believe they have no choice except to be possessed by their negative feelings. However, feelings cannot possess anyone. Instead, people possess their feelings, and they have many choices about how to respond.

It is not unusual for children whose parent figures act hysterical or "crazy" to decide not to show *any* feelings. They may be afraid that they will go crazy if they let go. It is also common for people to block their tears, fearing that if they start crying their tears will be a waterfall that never ends.

Many physical illnesses are created or made worse by negative feelings, by continuing stress, and by psychological problems. Psychotherapy may sometimes enhance a person's health and wellness. Some indications for psychotherapy are: intense anxiety, with sweating and faintness; sleep disturbance; substance abuse, including excessive use of alcohol; a sense of impending disaster; suspiciousness or fatigue when there seems to be no cause; obsessiveness; destructiveness to self, others or property; high irritability; accelerated speech or movement; confusion; loss of memory; inappropriate behavior or speech; apathy or impaired functioning. These symptoms, experienced at a fairly low level of intensity, are fairly common. When the symptoms interfere with a sense of freedom and an active search for happiness, professional help is needed.

For convenience, feelings can be grouped into four basic categories: mad, sad, scared, and happy. Children use words to talk about how they feel. More sophisticated words come later when vocabulary increases and nuances surface. Within each category of the mad, sad, scared, and happy words are many levels of intensity. For example, when people say they are mad at someone, the feeling may be frustration, which is a fairly low level of anger, or it may be rage, a much more intense level.

The value of expressing anger is often debated. When anger is released, more energy is available. Sometimes getting mad is a healthy response to a serious threat and may even be life-saving. Sometimes it is life-threatening.

Many professionals encourage the outward expression of anger because it is self-destructive when turned inward. Yelling while pounding pillows is a common therapeutic technique used to release hostile feelings. However, manipulation through anger is not uncommon. Persons who are easily angered often justify if on the grounds that it is effective. Like three-year-olds having temper tantrums to manipulate parents, they may get what they want in the short term. Most grown-ups eventually discover that it is not an effective way to increase their long-term happiness.

Based on personal or cultural values, most people believe they are entitled to get angry about certain things and are self-righteous in doing so. Whether or not they have the right, excess anger is often accompanied by feelings of guilt or depression. The new parent needs to recognize this and to set firm limits on the inner Child, so that rage is not expressed in destructive ways.

Sadness is another basic category, and can also be related to cultural values. For example, in some cultures people laugh at bad luck, in others they swear, in still others they cry. Sadness includes feelings such as grief, loneliness, despair, and depression. Sadness is debilitating, and when people experience it deeply they may withdraw physically or emotionally, thinking "I can't go on" or "I have nothing left to give" or "I don't want to live if it's going to be like this." Depression is the most widespread and serious form of sadness. Sometimes it has a biological or biochemical basis. Sometimes it is due to a negative view of oneself or the world. Depression can be caused by a conflict of values or the inability to make a decision. Also, people who are afraid of the intensity of their anger may find it safer to block it out and feel depressed.

Substituting one feeling for another usually occurs without any conscious effort. In any event, the basic problem remains unsolved. Whatever the cause, depression represents a depth of sadness that is the opposite of happiness, just as despair is the opposite of hope.

Grief is another form of sadness. It occurs whenever people experience a loss, and it is a natural response, especially after the loss of friends or family. In addition, the loss of some bodily function, a life-time dream, a job, a home, a pet, or a favorite possession often elicits sadness and grief.

When grieving, people experience physical symptoms of distress such as headaches, insomnia, loss of appetite, or stomach aches. They may feel panic because of inability to think. They may feel guilt, resentment, or hostility, and be unable to accomplish routine tasks.

Like sadness and grief, feeling scared also has levels of intensity ranging from apprehension through anxiety, fear, terror and panic. There is a natural apprehension before taking an exam or making an important speech or performing in some way that is subject to other people's judgment. Although some people are not apprehensive before these kinds of events, others experience anxiety or actual fear. Those who are most afraid may expect to be physically hurt, or judged inadequate. They believe that criticism will somehow reduce their personal strength and lower their self-esteem.

Anxiety is a generalized feeling, perhaps overall nervousness, rather than an identifiable specific feeling like fear. Anxiety can be a response to the past, the present, or the future. It often produces physical symptoms like tics, headaches, or agitation. A person may feel anxious without knowing why. Negative fantasies increase the anxiety level and can be overpowering. The person may be afraid of "falling apart". Some people ridicule themselves, or are ridiculed by others: "You dummy, there's nothing to be worried about."

Fear is more painful than anxiety. It is both more immediate and future-oriented. It occurs when there is an expectation that something very bad is going to happen. People with this expectation may also feel horror, loathing, dread, or panic.

Fear is a natural response to threatening situations. However, fear that was appropriate in the past is sometimes carried over into later life. When this occurs, people are fearful when there isn't anything to be afraid of. They may try to avoid any person or situation even remotely similar to what was feared in the past. If the fear becomes very intense, a person may experience overwhelming terror, collapse physically or emotionally, and become unable to cope with daily tasks or decide on long-range goals.

People who are frequently fearful, yet able to control it somewhat, go through life procrastinating to avoid making wrong choices. They may get mad at themselves or be sad for not being different. A potent new Parent is needed to protect the scared person (who might need to uncover the original sources of fear).

Everyone wants to feel happy oftener and for longer periods of time. Happiness has levels of intensity, just as the other basic feelings do. Satisfaction, contentment, and pleasure are at one level. Delight, elation, bliss, and ecstasy are at higher levels of intensity.

One of the characteristics of intense happiness is that it does not last. It either becomes less intense (though still pleasurable), or is negatively transformed. The transformation can be due to changes in the external situation, such as waking up happy then going to work and being fired. On the other hand, changes may be due to internal dynamics, such as being ill or even feeling guilty for being happy. It is the job of the new Parent to clear away the negative attitudes that prevent us from having more and more happiness in our lives.

Love works in many ways

Exercise: Recognizing Feelings

Following is a list of feelings many people experience. Check the ones that apply to you, how often you feel them, how the feelings affect your behavior, and how others respond to you.

Feelings I experience	Seldom? Occasionally? Frequently?	How my feelings affect my behavior	How others respond to me
Sad			
Grief			
Angry			
Ashamed			
Guilty			
Confused			
Inadequate			
Jealous			
Bored			
Anxious			
Scared			
Relaxed			
Lively			
Loving			
Excited			
Sexy			
Confident			
Free			
Happy			

Have some of these feelings become unpleasant habits that you want to change and don't know how? Perhaps your developing new Parent needs more education about feelings or needs to give you permission to have them.

Exercise: Redecisions and the New Parent

As you get acquainted with some of your childhood patterns about feeling and not feeling, begin to consider whether you need to make some redecisions.

• Sit down quietly. Take a few deep breaths and let your body and face relax. Release tension from your muscles. Loosen your jaw and lips, relax the muscles around your eyes, and let your breathing become slower.

• Imagine there is a TV screen in front of you and the story of your life is being played.

• Look closely at scenes where you are showing a lot of emotion.

• Then look at scenes where you are not showing the emotions you are actually feeling. Perhaps you are afraid to show how you feel or believe it won't do any good.

• Now look at any scenes that typically call for some emotional response, to which you are not responding either internally or externally.

As you consider these three kinds of scenes, do you think your new Parent needs to be more tender in encouraging you to redecide and really feel? Or do you need a firmer Parent, who will encourage you to experience your feelings in healthy, non-exploitive ways?

Tough Love/Tender Love

People need an internalized Parent who supports them in being and doing. Learning how to balance being and doing requires skill. Like a gymnast who knows the value of balance, a person in the process of self-reparenting needs a new Parent who will encourage both.

Unless both are encouraged and developed, happiness is always an elusive butterfly, just out of reach.

Sometimes, in childhood, *being* is stressed by adoring, overly nurturing parents. As a result, their children often feel entitled to everything they desire and are not motivated to establish goals that call for personal initiative or effort. They want what they want when they want it. They may become so self-centered that they need a new Parent who will use tough love.

People who have been overindulged, typically act on impulse and may be inconsistent or unreliable. They often undermine their own success by doing such things as speaking without thinking, acting without planning, or spending money without budgeting. They want to do what they want without regard for other people: want love without acting lovable, want happiness without commitment, want freedom without responsibility. These people need firm new Parents who will help them regulate their behavior.

The opposite type of person needs a tender new Parent. This is often true of those who have had brutal, overly strict, or highly critical parents who demanded perfect performance. These people need affirmation for *being* alive and being who they are, not just recognition for *doing* chores or school tasks.

Many people imagine they need tender, encouraging love when they may actually need tough love. You need tender, encouraging love if you were not affirmed for being you, and if you frequently experience a sense of despair or depression. You need firm, perhaps tough, love if your capacities for achievement, for independent thinking, and for action were not encouraged, if you act passive instead of assertive, or if you procrastinate often. When people identify whether they need tender or tough love, they take charge of their lives and take responsibility for their own happiness.

Exercise: Educating the Parent to Tenderness

Many people need to reparent themselves with a tender Parent who will encourage success and forgive failures, who will encourage relaxation and play and protest fear or overwork. Grade your symptoms.

Symptoms	Seldom	Sometimes	Frequently
• Can't think in stress			
• Panic if making a mistake			
• Depressed if not perfect			
• Scared of disapproval			
• Workaholic			
• Don't know how to play			
• Basically afraid			
• Basically anxious			

If you checked "frequently" more than any other category, you may need a tender Parent.

• If so, how can you begin the re-education?

• What could you do or say what would be effective for you?

Exercise: Educating the Parent to Firmness

Many people need to reparent themselves with a firm Parent who will not allow them to behave impulsively. Fill in the following, and decide if you need a firm Parent.

Symptoms	Seldom	Sometimes	Frequently
• Explode angrily			
• Get hysterical			
• Fall into depression			
• Eat or drink too much			
• Smoke when I shouldn't			
• Avoid exercising			
• Make promises I don't keep			
• Spend money I can't afford			
• Give advice without thinking			
• Act helpless when I'm not			
• Use movies, TV or telephone to avoid problems			
• Basically self-indulgent			
• Basically impulsive			

If you checked "frequently" the most, you may need a firm Parent in some areas of your life.

• If so, how can you begin this re-education?

• What could you do or say that would be effective for you?

Learning to Be Happy

The parent figures in your childhood may not have encouraged you to learn from a position of self-confidence. They may have given you the message that learning is tough work and that learning something new will always be a struggle. That's not necessarily true.

Relearning may be a challenge, even difficult. It's hard to relearn bad habits or teach yourself to be outgoing if you've been shy all your life. But too often we focus only on the first steps to learning something new, and those first steps are often the hardest! Look at the whole experience and you'll see that learning difficult things does not have to be agonizing or frustrating. It can be pleasurable. When you see progress, you'll feel both relief and satisfaction, which is often followed by happiness. Keep on educating your new Parent, and your new Parent will take good care of you. It won't be long before you can look beyond those difficult first steps to important signs of success, and happiness. Try it, you'll like it.

Happiness can be encouraged

5 Listening with Love

Have you ever said to yourself or someone else, "I wish I knew what I really wanted"?

Or have you ever said to yourself, "I'll never get what I need. Nobody cares. I might as well give up"?

Do you ever wonder how your life would be different if you could just find inner peace instead of turmoil?

Do you ever feel as if you're not put together in the right way, and you don't know what the right way is?

In this chapter the focus will be on discovering what your inner Child needs and wants. Knowing that, you can give yourself more freedom to be who you want to be and do what you want to do—more freedom to get on with your life and be happy. You cannot be truly happy until you have freed yourself from the past. It's never too late to start! You will need an awareness of how you shaped your needs and wants to please authority figures; how you learned to comply, rebel, or procrastinate; and how you may still do the same when you do not feel free.

The ability of any child to be creative, spontaneous, and self-directed, and to feel close to others, is usually directly affected by childhood authorities—parents, teachers, and others who have the power to design a situation that feels like a prison or one that feels like part of an open healthy world.

In this chapter you will learn how to enter into dialogue with your inner Child. This inner Child has much to tell you about specific needs and wants. With this knowledge you can begin to function as a liberating Parent who is able to encourage your pursuit of happiness.

How Needs and Wants Are Adapted

Children adapt their needs and wants to parents, parent figures, and their environment in many ways. They may argue and fight back, use delaying techniques if asked to help, or obey like "good" little boys or girls. These adaptions fall into three basic categories: compliance, rebellion and procrastination. Being compliant is usually based on the belief that obedience will bring love, or will at least decrease the chance of being punished. Being rebellious often happens because a child does not consider the parent's demands loving or rational. Procrastination is a wavering between the two: "Perhaps my parent will love me (or forgive me) if I eventually do what they want."

Although everyone uses all of these responses from time to time, a continuing pattern of procrastination and rebellion can become a major problem, both in childhood and in later life. Some parents punish children for this behavior. Others deal with it from a caring perspective, setting reasonable limits and reasonable consequences. Still other parents ignore rebelliousness and thus may encourage it— intentionally or not—and a child can become a tyrant. Tyrants are hard to love. They want total liberty for themselves and total obedience from others.

Many parents believe that one of their primary tasks is training their children to comply. The training may be indiscriminate, and thus destroy a child's sense of self-esteem. It may also be reasonable, and increase a child's sense of self-esteem. It may fluctuate at different times, for different reasons, around different subjects.

Parents teaching compliance usually justify their actions; they are "only doing their duty." But all too often they interpret their duty as the need to develop obedient children—in other words, "good" children who will not talk back, will not think independently, and who will not rebel against parental dictates.

Children who are taught compliance obey and without thinking have little capacity to make independent decisions in later life. As adults these people are easily swayed by others, are reluctant to take risks, and seldom question the system. They follow orders, even when the results may be bad for someone else or themselves.

Rebellion against authority often shows itself in early childhood if children feel unappreciated or unloved. First comes a sense of being treated unfairly. Next comes the decision, "I won't do what they want" or "I'll get even for what they did to me." The needs and wants of children are often just the opposite of those of their parents.

"I want you to pick up your toys," the parent might say. "I won't!" a child may respond. "Don't you dare talk to me like that!" may come next. The child's rebellion may then escalate outwardly into a temper tantrum or be withheld and built up internally as defiance.

Defiance is an attitude sometimes expressed in bold or insolent ways, sometimes in soft and procrastinating ways. Regardless of the mask it wears, defiance is an attempt to be free from authoritarian demands.

Parents respond differently to defiance. Some call it "stubbornness" and try to manipulate the stubborn child into obedience. Others may call it "guts," complimenting the child who takes that "try and make me" stance. Still other parents feel powerless and throw up their hands in dismay. In so doing they lose their ability to be adequate models and to influence their children effectively. They may love their children, but they don't know how to show it.

Rebellious children usually continue acting defiant in later life, even without cause. They are difficult to be with, since, when they don't get their way, they throw adult versions of their childhood temper tantrums. They are difficult to reach emotionally; their defiance acts as a barrier to love and intimacy.

Procrastination is what some children use against authorities when they want to rebel and don't want to comply. In procrastinating, they are trying to come to some kind of workable compromise that satisfies the inner war. Procrastination is a compromise, and "Just a minute" or "I'll do it later" is usually a safer way to ignore authorities and protect a sense of independence that directly saying no. Parents' behavior toward their children often fosters procrastination.

Procrastination is usually a slightly hidden form of rebellion. Children with demanding parents who frequently order "Do this," "Do that," may adapt by developing delaying techniques. Repressive parents who often say "Don't talk back" or "Don't ask so many questions" or "Shut up" may force their children to be quiet, go slow, and not ask for much. Such children need new messages of encouragement.

Sometimes procrastination can be a sign of a child who has not yet learned how to make decisions and is afraid of making a wrong one. Occasionally procrastination is used to manipulate others into taking on responsibility for the procrastinator or the procrastinator's assigned tasks. It is not unusual for the procrastinator to withdraw from loving relationships with others.

We are all familiar with the procrastinating adult! Who of us has not put off some unpleasant task? But serious procrastinators can be deeply troubled, and all procrastination usually has a hidden agenda. Immobilized by fear or acting out of repressed rebellion, the procrastinator appears to be trying, but is actually sabotaging his or her own life.

When people rebel, procrastinate or withdraw, it is often because they believe they are not lovable. When constantly criticized or told "no," this reinforces their belief. They may try to be perfect, or manipulate others to comply with their demands and, if not successful, feel frustrated and (sometimes) erupt into violence.

When these childhood patterns continue into adult life, change is needed. The person who complies a lot needs new Parent messages such as "You can think well for yourself," "You can decide what's right for you," "Set your own time schedule if you want to."

The person who is overly rebellious needs new Parent messages like "You can get what you want in better ways," "You don't have to have such a hot temper," and "Don't get so uptight about little things."

The person who procrastinates too often needs new Parent messages like "When you decide what you want, then go for it," "You don't have to make perfect decisions," and "If something goes wrong, you have the ability to straighten it out,"

It can be helpful to write your new Parent messages on 3×5 cards and put them in strategic places (on the bathroom mirror or the refrigerator door, or on your desk at work) where you're sure to see them often. These new messages become your own personal charter for happiness.

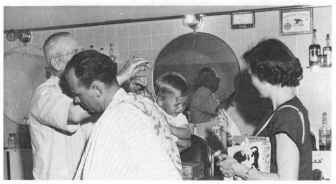

Responding to parental demands

Exercise: Your Response to Authority Then

Make a list of demands made on you in childhood, with your typical responses.

Childhood demands	How I complied	How I rebelled	How I procrastinated

How was your response to some authorities different from your response to others? Why do you suppose that was?

Exercise: Your Response to Authority Now

Make a list of demands currently being made on you by yourself or by others (spouse, parents, boss) and how you tend to respond.

Current demands	How I rebel	How I comply	How I procrastinate

• *How is your response to some authorities different from your response to others?*

• *What do you think is the reason for this?*

• *Is your response pattern similar to that of your childhood?*

• *What advice might a wise, loving new Parent give you?*

• *Would you rebel or procrastinate against the advice, or would you accept it?*

The Importance of Touch

The earliest adaptations that result in compliance, rebellion, and procrastination are partly related to the way children are touched when they are young. In severe cases parents beat their children, sexually molest them, or deny them food or other necessities to get them to obey. This may lead to external compliance, to rebellion (as when a child runs away), or to generalized insolence, generated by rage that is held back temporarily. This rage may later be expressed as brutality toward people or pets who are weaker. It may also be expressed hurtfully toward oneself. Hating or hurting one's body—or an insatiable craving to be touched—often has its beginnings in unhealthy touch or lack of touch in childhood. Even in "normal" families many parents have a hard time expressing their love with physical gestures or loving behavior.

If lovingly cared for, children will respond with love. The responsive smiles and wiggles of infants show that humans are equipped at birth for healthy relationships and intimacy. Frequent touching, rocking, carrying, and holding all stimulate an infant's well-being. Without sufficient touching, infants become sick, even die. For maximum mental and physical health, healthy loving touch is an absolute necessity. This is just as true when you become an adult. As you begin to know the needs and wants of your inner Child, you may discover fear of some kinds of touch and longing for others.

The importance of touch begins at birth. The first gasp for breath, the shock of cooler air and bright lights can be made easier by the caressing of human hands. Liberation from the protective womb into a world that is not always protective is an event of great magnitude. Infants who are not separated from their mothers immediately seem to have a greater sense of trust about the world around them.

Contact comfort with softness and warmth is the most important variable in the famous Harlow studies of monkey behavior. The studies show that laboratory monkeys separated from their own mothers at birth selected soft cloth mother-surrogates for contact comfort, even though a wire-mesh surrogate could feed them. In like manner, infants cling to the softness of their mothers and, if they are not available, are often happy with a soft blanket or toy.

Later in life, softness in another person may be preferred to harshness. Interestingly enough, when people increase the amount of soft and loving touch they give and receive, their faces often soften, and frequently they look years younger.

A loving touch stimulates growth

Exercise: Your Touch Portrait

This exercise is designed to help you discover how and where you like to be touched or don't like to be touched. Probably it is related to your childhood.

Draw two full-length portraits of yourself in the accompanying frames. Make one a front view and one a back view.

• Fill in with little whirls or circles the parts of you that were lovingly touched in childhood.

• Leave blank those parts of you that were seldom or ever touched in childhood.

• Make crisscross lines where you were touched in embarrassing or hurting ways.

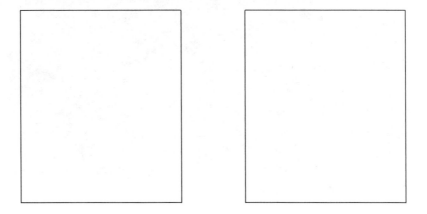

As you consider your portraits, what are the implications for your life now? What does your inner Child need from a healthy new Parent?

Exercise: Current Touch Patterns

As you think of your childhood and how you were touched,
consider your preferences in your current life.

Many families and other cultural groups have customs about how
physically close people should be, including how to shake hands,
and how often; how to kiss, hug, or have sex, and how often; how
to touch or not touch children; and so forth.

What are some of the beliefs and patterns you have about touch
and how did you develop them?

Touching I like or am comfortable with	How I learned this	Touching I dislike or am uncomfortable with	How I learned this

Is there anything you want to change about what you like or dislike?
If so, what can you begin to do?

Sometimes I Feel Like a Motherless Child

Being physically or emotionally forced into compliance is an intrusion that interferes with the growth of self-esteem. Without self-esteem, and the permissions and protections that encourage it, some children feel they have no parents—that they have been abandoned. It's impossible, then, to feel happy.

Being abandoned by a parent leaves a terrible scar, and feeling like a motherless or fatherless child may be re-experienced in adulthood when things go wrong. Whatever the inadequacies of the parents, there is still a yearning to believe that some things about the parents were positive, and that their inadequacies were due to circumstances in their own childhood over which they had no control. All of us need to be comforted when things go wrong, and if our parents are dead or our friends do not act in caring ways, the feeling of being motherless or fatherless can be overwhelming. The old spiritual "Sometimes I feel like a motherless child a long way from home" touches the wellsprings of many who hunger or thirst for a loving parent.

Exercise: Music to Remember

Have you ever found yourself humming a song over and over, and suddenly realized that what you were humming reflected an unsolved problem? Maybe the song was to give you the courage to take action, or to move you from depression to hope, or to remind you that you are lovable. In similar ways, the music you heard when you were growing up may have influenced you.

What were some of the lullabys or other songs you heard frequently when you were little?

Did you ever feel like a motherless child and have a song that reflected the feeling?

What were some you chose to hear most often in your high-school years? As a young adult?

Were the songs romantic? Nostalgic? Stirring? Pious? Fun? Tearful? Patriotic? Inspirational? Liberating or enslaving?

What might you learn from this?

Who Is Listening?

The main reason so many people feel motherless or fatherless is that those parents were absent by reason of death, desertion, divorce or just emotional disinterest. The most common way disinterest is expressed is in not listening. Children need and want to be heard. Many people feel that they were not listened to enough when they were little or, if listened to, were not understood.

One of the skills important to self-reparenting is listening to your own inner Child. Children who are not really listened to may give up trying to be heard, withdraw, and become loners. Or they may become depressed and mumble, as if what they have to say isn't important. In contrast, some children who do not get listened to decide to act in rebellious or aggressive ways. Desperate for attention, they may do almost anything to get it.

People tend to have conversations going on inside their heads so constantly that they may not be aware of them. Sometimes they hear a parental reprimand for not having said or done certain things "correctly." Sometimes it is parental encouragement. Sometimes it is a lament of the Child, or a repetition of a childhood decision like "I really hate him, and I'm going to get even" or "I'm so scared I don't know what to do" or "I can't stand being alone; I feel like I'm going crazy" or "I'll never make it." Learning to listen to this sub-vocal talking is very important in self-reparenting.

There are many advantages to learning how to listen to self talk. Learning how to listen to the internal parent-child arguments may clarify inner conflicts, ambiguities, or incongruencies. Learning how to listen to the child's defensive statements and excuses can reveal unmet needs and wants. Learning how to listen to one's body and its SOS signals for more rest or exercise, more food or less, more loving care and less neglect, can actually be life-saving.

Exercise: Being Listened To

Go back to your childhood and to various situations when you had something to say and wanted people to listen to you.

When I wanted to say something	Responses from parent figures	What I said to myself

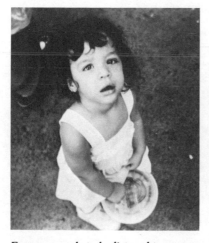 

Everyone needs to be listened to

Now consider your current life and whether people listen to you.

When I want to say something	Responses from parent figures	What I say to myself

Is there any similarity between the way people listen to you now and the way they did when you were young?

When There Are No Words

Since everyone was once an infant, and may occasionally respond to life experiences totally at the feeling level—nonverbally, with cries, screams, or gurgles of delight.

Such regression can occur during times of stress or crisis, when a person may feel helpless, unable to think or even talk. Reliving traumatic childhood experiences, perhaps in trance or hypnotic states, may also induce regression. At such times the person may feel totally incapacitated and unable to take appropriate action.

The child who has no words needs an inner Parent who is encouraging and supportive instead of critical or sadistic. During the time when the new Parent is being constructed, the rational, clear-thinking Adult part of the personality must be in charge. It must not seem to be going away and abandoning the Child. The inner Child will know if that occurs and will return to its previous unhappy state.

To avoid this, a person's Adult needs to be in continuing contact with the Child. Sometimes it helps people to hold a pillow in their arms and rock it back and forth while cooing baby talk. This is an aid to the Child, who begins to experience (or re-experience) much-needed nurturing and the support of a loving new Parent.

Needs and Wants Are Not the Same

Freedom to experience the creative and happy Child within depends on whether that Child's needs and wants are lovingly heard. Survival usually depends on having physical needs met. People experience these needs as absolute: "I'm so thirsty I can't stand it" or "I'm so cold I feel as though I'm freezing to death" or "I'm so tired I feel like collapsing." Physical needs can often be satisfied by some object or action: a drink, a sweater, a nap, or food.

Wants are different. Getting what you want is seldom necessary for survival, yet is often desired to improve the quality of life. Wants are wishes to have something that is missing or to have something more. Wanting can be intense, especially for those who experience emotional deprivation. For them it may become a survival need.

The words *want* and *need* are often used interchangeably. "I really *need* to go out to dinner tonight" may in fact be "I *want* to go out to dinner tonight because I don't want to cook." "I *want* to go to bed early" may instead be "My body really *needs* rest."

The energy people put into pleasing themselves and getting what they want may be more or less than they use to satisfy their needs. In affluent, consumer-oriented societies, some people may be so satisfied that they do not distinguish between the two.

When people give up hope, they cease to want. Instead of wanting something to be different and being motivated to do something about it, they begin to daydream, or they give up even the fantasy and resign themselves to unhappiness.

People who do not like themselves, or who imagine no one else could like them, may deny their own wants or ignore their own needs. Those who do not like or respect other people will also believe that others do not have the right to get their needs or wants met.

Getting needs and wants met is important. Happiness increases when this occurs.

Exercise: Confronting Fear

When people decide to ask others for what they need and want, or when they decide to go after it themselves, they often hold back because of fear. It could be a fear of disapproval or a fear of abandonment; these are the most common holdovers from childhood. Other people fear failure—or success! Still others have a fear of finding out who they really are. This exercise is to help you discover it you have some expectations that interfere with your pursuit of happiness.

Needs and wants I have that I don't pursue	Catastrophic expectations that hold me back	How I could get help from my potent new Parent

Some catastrophic expectations are like phobias. If you feel very stuck with one of yours, you can learn in the next chapter how to desensitize your fears.

Exercise: Positive Action Plans

Like most people, you probably have some catastrophic expectations *about your life and health, your success and failures, your capacity to cope with loss, your inability to get total approval from others, and so forth.*

This exercise is to focus your attention on *serious* possibilities *that you tend to avoid thinking about and therefore have no action plans for them. How about changing this now in a positive way?*

Natural, international and personal crises that I avoid thinking about	Possible action plans for each of these crises

Exercise: Yes, You Can!

Sometimes you may feel that you won't be able to follow your plan in a crisis. Yet intellectually you know that you can. You know this because: you are currently solving problems; in the past you have often solved problems; you plan to think in the future, not only about solving problems, but also about how to continue your pursuit of happiness.

In this exercise, write yourself a letter in three parts. Spend time on it. It is important, like an insurance policy.

• In part one, compliment yourself for problems you solved in the past by thinking them through.

• In part two of your letter, compliment yourself for the thinking you are doing now in your current life. Be specific about your compliments.

• In part three, compliment yourself for being able to predict that you will be able to think even better in the future.

Now file your letter some place where you will be able to find it easily in a crisis.

Exercise: "What Do You Want? What Do You Need?"

This is one of the most important exercises in the entire process of self-reparenting. It will be a dialogue between your Child and your Adult. Your Adult will act as a nurturing Parent to discover what your Child needs or wants.

First, find a quiet place and get in a comfortable position. Let your eyelids drop; let your body go limp.

Imagine you as a child sitting beside you as a grown-up. See yourselves in a pleasant setting such as a quiet park surrounded by flowers, or the seashore where the sun is pleasant and the surf is quiet, or the mountains where the air is fresh and the sounds and smells are natural.

Speak internally to yourself as a child, using a loving, supportive voice and manner. Use an endearing term or affectionate name, as a parent might with a child, and ask yourself:

"What do you want?"

"What do you need?"

Continue to use the two questions several times and listen for your inner Child answers. Encourage the inner dialogue.

Withhold all judgment at this time on whether what you want and need is good for you. Remember, good parents listen well.

List your Child's wants and needs. Don't evaluate; just list them.

My Child Needs	My Child Wants

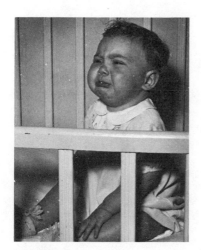

Many needs and wants

Exercise: Justice and the Ideal Parent

The ideal parent is deeply concerned with the justice of a child's needs and wants. In this exercise you will refer to the previous one. List the same wants and needs, and let your ideal Parent judge whether what you want and needs is appropriate and possible.

Needs and wants I currently have	Advice my ideal parent would give me	Action I could take

Now check each of your needs and wants:

+   if you intend to start doing something about it now

−   if it is impossible or inappropriate now

?   if you want to evaluate it more before deciding

Born to Love

Everyone hopes to be loved, and many people's hopes are realized. Love is life-giving: it heals, it liberates, and it is intense, durable, and unconditional. It is capable of sacrifice if needed and is without exploitation. It is good will freely given, asking nothing in return.

Attachment is not the same as love. People are often legally or emotionally attached to others they do not even like. It is a tragedy when there is no love between parents and their children. Children are born to love.

Unfortunately, for a variety of reasons parents may treat their children so that the children do not feel lovable or loving. Disliking and even hating themselves, these children can get into patterns of self-destructiveness or lash out to inflict damage on objects or pets or people. Those who experience too much physical or emotional pain do not believe in the miracle of love. They need to be healed with the kind of love that gives them protection and permission. If this healing succeeds, it can release their capacity to be loving and allow them to claim the birthright of being loved.

Parents who expect appreciation or high performance from children as payment for "loving" them pollute the relationship, much as clear water can be polluted. The new internal Parent must be able to love without exploiting the inner Child.

Love Is Action

People can endure almost any catastrophe if they know they are lovable and if they are able to show love to others. Love is not just warm feelings; love is action. Parents who love a child intensely take care of its body, mind, and spirit and encourage the child to treat them with respect. A good parent needs to love so intensely that he or she willingly sacrifices time and energy because of love. This parent

and caring for the Child is always a high priority. Thus, when the child has an important need or want, the loving parent rearranges priorities to deal with it. This is especially important when the child is young and requires intense involvement.

Later in life, the one-to-one intensity needs to be transformed so that the child can learn to love more extensively. Many people talk of loving everything and everybody, yet they may not show it. Others only love themselves and one or two others. Between the extremes can be a healthy balance. In self-reparenting, a new Parent needs to know that every person is important—that love is not a scarce commodity, and there is enough love to go around.

Love in action may be brief, as when someone briefly risks his or her own life for another and doesn't wait for thanks. Or love may be a lifelong relationship, as in some marriages or friendships. Good parents make this permanent commitment to their children as persons, even though they may not agree with some of their values or lifestyles. In self-reparenting, a person's new Parent must have a similar orientation, which is to stay active, never to desert the inner Child, and always to show love—no matter what.

Adequacy of parental love can be measured in two ways: loving involvement and parenting skills. Some parents who love their children and are emotionally involved with them do not have adequate parenting skills. For example, they may be overly indulgent of inappropriate behavior or overly indulgent by trying to give their children "everything." As a result, their children often become spoiled, act irresponsible with possessions, or manipulate others dishonestly to get more. Most of this behavior occurs because the parents are inadequate in parenting skills and unwise in gift-giving.

Another inadequacy in parental care is when parents do *not* love their children and are emotionally distant, even though they may have parenting skills. They do not enjoy the positive emotional involvement with their children that comes about while learning and working, playing and loving together. They do their parenting out of a sense of duty, or so they will look good in the eyes of the neighbors.

Whether parents are loving and uninformed, or informed and unloving, the result is similar because the parenting is inadequate. In developing your new Parent, you will need to decide to love your inner Child just because the Child is important, and to love so much that the Child becomes free to love others. Your own Child needs to be loved permanently and unconditionally, regardless of mistakes and imperfections. And your inner Child needs the wisdom of loving concern combined with firmness. When people are loved, they can learn to love themselves and the rest of the world and experience liberty and happiness at the deepest levels. They can become friends with the universe.

The root of the word *friend* means "free"—not in bondage, noble, glad. The Old Englilsh word *freon* means to love, and the word *freoud* becomes the modern English word *friend*. In the process of self-reparenting, the new Parent does not hold the Child in bondage. Instead, the Parent respects the nobility and the mobility of the Child, and rejoices over its emerging independence. The two of them becomes friends.

Exercise: "Lovable? Who, Me?"

Sit back, relax your shoulders, and re-experience the ways you were loved in childhood by your parents or parent substitutes. Then fill in the following.

Times I knew I was loved	Times I doubted I was loved	How the love and non-love showed	Ways I could love myself more

What commitments do I need to make to myself?

Am I willing to do this?

If so, when?

If not, why not?

Listen with Love

Love can be compared with water. Everybody needs it and wants it. Like an ocean, love can have depth. Like a storm at sea, it can have intensity. Like a storm at sea, it can have intensity. Like a still pond in a meadow, it can be quiet. Like a quickly moving mountain stream, it can be pure. Like the power from a waterfall, it can energize. Love not only quenches thirst, but it can also wash clean.

The continuing task of your new Parent will be to love. It must ask, time and time again, "What do you need? What do you want?" Then, listening with love, the new Parent will accept some over-compliance, rebellion, procrastination and withdrawal and encouragingly remind your inner Child of your own action-based program for happiness.

6 The Power to Be Happy

Do you ever catch run around acting as if happiness, in the form of a person, is just around the corner?

Do you ever drive yourself for more and more money, believing it will be the doorway to happiness?

Do you ever struggle for more recognition, believing that if you get it you will be more important and consequently happier?

Do you ever look forward with excitement to your time off work so you can play or relax or try a new hobby that will give you happiness?

If so, you know the enjoyment of pursuit. You like setting goals and you pursue them with a sense of hope. You expect your achievements to bring you happiness, and sometimes they do. Other times, when you achieve your goals you may find that your world has changed in some way and your achievements now seem irrelevant, failing to bring the glow you anticipated. Then you may ask yourself "What was it all about?", "Why did I put in all that time and energy on something that doesn't really matter?"

Happiness by Legislation

The Declaration of Independence of the United States of America proclaims there are "certain unalienable rights, that among these are life, liberty and the pursuit of happiness." It goes on to say that the principles and powers of a government should be derived from the consent of the people and should be in a form most likely to effect safety and happiness.

Happiness was again legislated in 1787 when the Constitution of the United States of America was signed and two years later the Bill of Rights, which were the first ten amendments to the Constitution, was approved. In the Bill of Rights was the reaffirmation of the rights of "life, liberty and the pursuit of happiness."

In 1948 the General Assembly of the United Nations adopted the Universal Declaration of Human Rights as a standard for all people and nations. This document affirmed that equal and inalienable rights for all people are essential to freedom, justice and peace and that international order is necessary for these rights and freedoms to be realized.

In comparing the United Nations and the U.S.A. statements of inalienable "rights," it is interesting that the "pursuit of happiness" is part of the U.S.A. tradition and not part of the United Nations statement. Perhaps food or economic stability has been a higher priority to many nations and they believe happiness would be the logical outcome of freedom, justice and peace.

Although the "pursuit of happiness" is legislated in the U.S.A., the achievement of happiness is not. The implication is that even the process of pursuing something has great validity, and people are entitled to hope for success as they engage in the pursuit.

In this chapter you will discover that you have within you the power to be happy. You will learn more about your natural human needs for power, how these needs and desires may have been thwarted at one time, and how they can now be released. The pursuit of happiness is a natural and constitutional right.

Others may make it easier

Exercise: Your Pursuit of Happiness

Consider the various times in your childhood, adolescence, and adulthood when you hoped for and actively pursued specific goals that you believed would make you happy. Perhaps you reached your goals, perhaps you didn't. Write about the times you recall, using the following chart.

Goals I have had	Methods I used to reach them	I succeeded or did not	Effect on my life

• *When you recall your goals and your pursuit of them, was it the achievements that were important, or was it the pursuit that you enjoyed?*

• *How long did your pleasure last?*

• *Are there implications for your life now?*

Developing Personal Power

There are many developmental theories regarding personality, although we don't yet have fully developed and widely tested theories
that take into account sexual and cultural differences. Erik Erikson's
developmental theory is one of these based solely on the male personality, yet it is still very useful as a general guide. Erikson's concept
is that particular powers (he calls them *virtues*) develop at specific age
levels if people solve the basic crisis associated with that age. These
powers are hope, will, purpose, competence, fidelity, love, care, and
wisdom.

People who experience these powers have solved some basic crises
that are part of growing up. People who lack these powers have failed
to solve some of the basic crises. Some people seem to jump a stage
or two and lack one strength, yet have the next one. When that is the
case, they are like a building with a weak foundation that may break
up in a big storm.

The Power of Hope

The first developmental crisis that confronts each infant between birth
and one-and-a-half years old is trust versus mistrust of parents. If
nurturing, warm, affectionate care is given, if the immediate environment and the parent figures are experienced as dependable, children
learn to trust and consequently are optimistic. They become hopeful
because their earliest significant persons are reliable and caring.

Hope is the virtue or power that develops from the successful resolution
of the internal conflict about whether it is safe to trust parents. Hope
is the belief that certain wishes are attainable in spite of everything.
Once established as part of the personality of the child, hope can
sustain a person even when trust seems unrealistic. The capacity to
hope is at the center of being human. It is a feeling or belief that
solutions to most problems are possible and that dreams for a better
future have a chance of being realized.

When people are without hope, they lose interest in the future and often lose energy to face even simple daily tasks. Of course, some things cannot be changed no matter how high the hope. At a time like that, trusting persons, in spite of unhappiness, still hope to make the best of the situation.

Some people are overly trusting. They see the world through rose-colored glasses. Life may have been "ideal" when they were little, so they trust everyone and continue to trust them when clear evidence shows some people are not trustworthy. Gullible and naive, unwilling to think critically about a person or situation, these people may collapse when they finally acknowledge one's lack of trustworthiness.

People who did not gain a basic sense of trust in infancy, so that they can experience the power of hope, may go through life feeling incomplete, empty, and distrustful of others. Some do experience basic trust early in life but, in the process of growing up, lost it because of some tragedy or crisis. These people often go through life feeling deeply lonely, wondering whether it is ever safe to trust again.

The inability to trust often leads to a pervading sense of depression that interferes with the healthy development. For example, when children are ignored, seldom touched, brutalized, or starved, they may not mature at a normal rate. Children who are abandoned (whether the abandonment is due to death or desertion) also may lack the strength to trust and hope.

In later life such people expect others to ignore them, be cruel to them, or be untrustworthy in some other way. Because of this underlying fear, they may cling to someone who is actually trustworthy and then act in such negative ways so that the other person leaves out of desperation. Or they may cling to someone from an overly dependent position that restricts their own freedom to develop autonomy.

Exercise: Learning to Hope

Perhaps you can remember what your parents and parent figures, and home and school environments were like when you were very young, whether you could trust them or not, and what you hoped for or gave up hoping for.

People who were trustworthy	Ways they showed it	How it affected me

People who were not trustworthy	Ways they showed it	How it affected me

What I hoped for as a child	What happened to my hopes	How it affected me

Hoping for acceptance

The Power of Will

The necessary dependence during the first year-and-a-half of life begins to moderate as children moving toward age three become aware of their emerging autonomy through their growing power to use their bodies. They discover they don't need to be carried; they can walk and do many other things on their own. They discover their will, and the power of their will.

Children of this age are very ambivalent. They often do not want to let mother out of sight, yet they want to be independent when she is around. Along with this conflict between the urge for autonomy and the lingering inability to be autonomous comes self-doubt and shame for not being able to do things without help and for crying or "acting like a baby." In many families boys are encouraged to be independent and girls are not. Both may be shamed by their parents if they act autonomous.

Shame is experienced as a diffused sense of anxiety, self-doubt as not living up to a fantasized ideal. Both feelings are based on a decision that "I am weak or inadequate." This is toilet-training time, so it is not surprising that shame is often described as feeling exposed, "caught with my pants down." If the crisis of autonomy, versus shame and self-doubt, is not resolved, patterns of helplessness develop. Fear of trying new experiences may plague these people throughout life. This is not at all unusual with those who were hospitalized as young children. Their urges for physical independence and autonomy were severely restricted by hospital procedures, and their sense of safety threatened when mother was not available.

If the crisis is successfully resolved, the strength to pursue happiness with less anxiety and more autonomy is developed. "I will do it," says the child. Developing a sense of will is crucial to breaking free and to achieving liberty. Will is determination to act in spite of self-doubt, in spite of shame that may be experienced if something is not done perfectly. The will acts as a self-organizing urge to set goals and motivate people to achieve them.

Children who are over-organized by their parents may not learn how to recognize and use their wills. Later in life, their will is weak rather than strong. Either passively or anxiously they may wait for destiny, or fate, or for some real or imagined authority to direct their lives. Even when their very existence is threatened, as in an earthquake or fire or when seriously ill or hurt, they may not know how to call on this inner power.

The power of the will is not the same as the will to power. The power of the will is based on using personal strength to take charge of one's own life. It is striving to do well and actualizing one's own potentials. The will to power is based on efforts to take charge of someone else's life. It shows in one of two ways. A person may strive for power over others from a position of superiority (trying to be better than anyone else) in a class, on a job, in appearance, in social life. This person often shows high ambition or self-righteousness and uses power over others like a controlling parent. The opposite type is the person who tries to control others by helplessness. This person may feel anxious and inadequate and thus act shy or weak, use poor judgment, or try to get others to make decisions. By acting helpless, this person also uses power—to manipulate others into caretaking roles.

Exercise: Your Will and Your Will to Power

As a young child you were either encouraged or restricted from developing your will, which is the natural urge for independence and autonomy. How was this development encouraged or restricted?

My attempts at autonomy	Encouraged or restricted	How I felt them	Effect in my life

Decision making and will power

As a child you also tried to exert your will to power over others by some form of manipulation such as tears or temper tantrums. What was the result?

How I tried to control others	How I succeeded or failed	How I felt them	The effect of my efforts

As you study your childhood patterns for using your will, are you satisfied? If not, what new-Parent messages do you need that could decrease your self-doubt and increase your independence?

The Power of Purpose

During ages three to six, interest begins to shift from wanting autonomy to concern for "Who am I (as a boy or a girl)?" Awareness of one's sexual identity becomes important. Boys tend to seek their mother's attentions; girls may act to get their fathers to notice them. Parents are often confused by a son's remark that "I'm going to marry

Mama when I grow up" or, from a daughter, "I wish Mama would go away so I could have Daddy to myself." This is a difficult crisis for children who were not born the "right" sex to please their parents. They are in the process of deciding what kind of person to be and developing a sense of purpose for living. They want to set goals and achieve them.

When children's efforts at self-understanding and goal setting are misunderstood, punished or ridiculed, they experience guilt. Guilt is not the same as shame. Shame is more likely to stem from a sense of inferiority at not being able to be autonomous. Guilt is experienced as not being able to please others. If a person often takes initiative and is disapproved, then the power to set goals that have purpose and meaning may be suppressed or seriously damaged.

When a child hears messages like "I'll decide what you should do and you better obey me," he or she may experience extreme feelings of guilt for breaking even minor rules. Children may stop thinking for themselves if they are criticized when they do so. They may develop a compulsive need to please others, and the "others" may not be willing to be pleased by anything less than perfection. Thus the purposeful goal-setting urges that develop in preschool years may be thwarted or distorted. For this person, goals that are self-determined may be difficult to decide upon in later life.

If the crisis of initiative versus guilt is resolved, however, then a person is able to take more initiative without feeling guilty, even if the initiated action is far from perfect. These people have a sense of *purpose* and know the power of it, and they have a conscience about using it. Life has meaning. Happiness is discovered through using the power of purpose to set and achieve realistic goals.

Exercise: From Guilt to Goal Setting

*All children try to take initiative in various ways as they grow up.
This is especially important between three and six years old. When
not encouraged, children often feel guilty and begin to accept goals
that please others instead of pleasing themselves.*

How I took initiative	Parent response	Effect on me

In your current life, consider your goals, the purposes they serve in your life, and the initiative you take to achieve these goals.

How I took initiative	Parent response	Effect on me

In developing your new Parent, do you need encouragement to go for your goals? If so, what specific message do you need to give yourself?

The Power of Competence

Between the ages of seven and twelve, the crisis of mastery versus inferiority emerges. The need for mastery arises in two areas. There is a need to master academic challenges, and a corresponding need to master social challenges.

Mastery in academics is possible during these years because children are developmentally ready for active learning and are able to focus their attention. They are also more capable of social success at this age. All-boy groups and all-girl groups are typical. There is more freedom from home control and more chance to learn how to interact with others.

Children who are not successful in their efforts to master the academic and social challenges usually experience a painful sense of inferiority when they are out in the world. They feel very awkward instead of competent. If they feel awkward, they may withdraw from interaction with peers and become loners, using their time as bookworms or TV addicts. Later in life such a person may have few (or no) friends, may work at something that calls for being alone, and may continue to feel inferior to others and not know what to do about it.

Some children who feel inferior begin to act in aggressive or delinquent ways, cutting school or failing academically. Later they may continue delinquent behavior. Children who succeed socially and fail academically may continually seek out others. They may feel incompetent at making independent choices unless doing so with others who are willing to lead while they follow.

Building a sense of competence can be very difficult. For example, the person who feels inferior in mathematics may need to develop an appreciation for sports abilities or interests in various hobbies. The person who feels inferior in interpersonal relations may need to join some kind of program that provides opportunities for a gradual emerging of social skills. People whose intelligence is at near-genius level sometimes decide to focus their interests in areas in which they are most competent. They may recognize, painfully, that the number of people they can relate to at an intense intellectual level is not as high as they wish.

The freedom of self-confidence

Exercise: From Inferiority to Competence

*Between the ages of seven and twelve, you may have felt competent
in some situations and incompetent or inferior in others. In this
exercise explore how you handled the basic academic and social
challenges.*

Academic challenges in childhood	Mastered them or didn't	How I felt and acted	Effect on my life

Social challenges in childhood	Mastered them or didn't	How I felt and acted	Effect on my life

Now consider your current intellectual and social challenges and note whether they are related to your childhood urge for independence. How can a new Parent help you now?

Current challenges	How they are related or not to childhood	How my new Parent could help me

The Power of Fidelity

To affirm one's own identity and be loyal to it is the task for persons between the ages of twelve and eighteen. Unless this is done, a person may experience years of identity diffusion. Adolescence is also a time when young people question traditional values and ask ideological questions about the meaning of life. The process of questioning values naturally includes questioning self-identity: "Am I a valuable person?" "Is it permissible to be who I am?" "Do I know who I am, or am I confused about my identity?"

One of the major reasons this period is so difficult, especially in some parts of the Western world, is that many adolescents are kept dependent—by law, society and parents—for an over-extended period of time. Their opportunities for growing up and taking their place in the adult world is restricted.

The sense of identity diffusion, "I don't know who I am," is a continuing problem if this crisis is not resolved. Drug abuse is only one sign that a healthy personal identity has not been achieved. Unwillingness to take responsibility for one's feelings and behavior is another. Blaming others is a third way. It implies that the blamer is outside the situation and not responsible for what goes wrong. Personal pleasure, regardless of its effect on others, may then become the major goal in life. A person's sexuality matures during those years, yet the capacity for authentic and caring love—for a partner or for children—may not develop because of identity diffusion and confusion.

Adolescence is a time in life when bodies and sexual urges are changing so rapidly that young people often feel confused about who they are and the values and people that they want to remain faithful to. Rituals such as bar mitzvahs that recognize this stage in life are important. So, too, are parents who are confirming, not exploiting, and friends who are also affirming. Joining clubs, getting married, and developing close friends are usually efforts in this direction.

When a firm sense of identity is established during these years, the power of fidelity is also established. This power is the ability to remain loyal in spite of value contradictions that are sometimes confusing. Fidelity is necessary for the next step, which is learning how to move into an authentic love relationship that is affirming, not confusing. Without a strong sense of identity and the power of fidelity that results from this sense, feelings of loneliness and separation from the entire world may become overwhelming. Love may seem elusive, something at the end of a rainbow and always out of reach.

Fidelity is learning to love

Exercise: From Identity Confusion to Self-Affirmation

Between the ages of twelve and eighteen you probably felt comfortable about yourself in some ways and not in others. Of course, you may have changed your mind during those years, yet as you evaluated yourself you were also sorting out what you considered to be your unique identity.

Areas of concern	Disliked or confused	Somewhat uncomfortable	Comfortable and accepting
My body or clothes			
My face or hair			
My capacity to think			
My friendships			
My love relationships			
My home environment			
My skills in sports			
My skills in music			
My skills in			

If during your teenage years you were not comfortable with yourself, have you gained this comfort since then?

If you have not, what do you need from a healthy new Parent that will help you?

The Power of Love

Intimacy versus isolation is the next developmental crisis. It is related to unresolved issues around trust or nontrust which begin to surface again between ages 18 and 30. "Dare I trust someone enough to be truly intimate, or shall I withdraw and insulate myself instead?" "Am I important enough so that someone will come if I need them?" "Will they accept me as I am with all my unresolved needs." "If I love other people, will they eventually leave me?"

One of the mistakes many people make when they form intimate relations with others is to expect the other person to be trustworthy in every area of life 100 percent of the time. That is seldom, if ever, the case. Everybody makes promises to themselves and others, and everybody breaks some of their promises. This happens by intent or by accident, and when it does one person usually defends and justifies by offering a "reason" for the broken promise. The other person defends and justifies their anger or despair. "I just couldn't help it" is a widely heard plea for forgiveness. "But you promised!" is the widely heard retort and plea for commitment.

The capacity to love with a mutual devotion that can endure and reduce normal differences of opinions and antagonisms grows more readily if the earlier trust issues of birth to one-and-a-half years old have been resolved. Strongly based on awareness of personal identity and commitment to fidelity, love, as it develops between 18 and 30, is selective and often experienced as a shared identity. Without love, life seems empty and hopeless, and loneliness seems inevitable.

People speak of love in many ways. They say they are "falling in love" or "falling out of love" or they speak of "making love" or "losing love." They speak of loving their cat or dog, their garden or car, their children, their spouse. However people may speak of it or define it, love is usually recognized as an intense emotion that gives pleasure and delight when it is reciprocal and leads to agony when it is not.

Love is often confused with romance, although it is not the same. Romantic love is usually short-term and an exaggeration of emotional highs and lows. It is somewhat manic-depressive. It's like being on a roller coaster going up to the peak of excitement then dropping suddenly. This kind of love can have a high cost.

Real love is more comprehensive. It may also have highs and lows, yet underneath both feelings is a steady current of trust and appreciation. Between some people, love involves sexual desire. Always it includes unconditional good will and the yearning for closeness that is part of intimacy. Love protects from the sadness of isolation and the terror of abandonment.

The freedom to be oneself, the happiness when sharing confidences and interests, is lovingly experienced in the context of friendship. The happy person is one who counts both family and non-family members as friends and takes time and effort to cultivate and encourage the growth of friendships. Whereas idealism, romanticism, and adventure characterize friendships in youth, the reinforcing cement of love, without possessiveness, characterizes more mature relationships. In non-possessive relationships people keep their own identities and encourage others to do the same.

Because life without love reinforces negatives, it is important to assess one's friendships. Some people remain friends with others only if it is to their financial, social, or emotional advantage. Knowingly or unknowingly, they use others and, in the using, are often abusive of what the friend has to give. This is not friendship; it may give some mutual satisfaction, but the satisfaction is usually temporary. Eventually the relationship begins to feel restrictive or boring to those involved, often because it has been based on use instead of on love.

Exercise: From Loneliness to Love

Loneliness is painful. It is first experienced in infancy. Usually it is due to being isolated or ignored. When children's needs are not met, parent and child intimacy does not develop, and the child does not learn how to trust. Mistrust and loneliness become unpleasant yet familiar feelings. In later life loneliness, being familiar, is often expected. Intimacy may be avoided or restricted because of a basic lack of trust.

Consider your life between the ages of 18 and 30 and look for patterns. If you are older, consider other relationships as well, and how they are similar or different to those you had as a young adult.

Persons I wanted to be close to	What I did to encourage or deter intimacy	The emotional effect on me

- *If you have a habit of getting close to people, then breaking apart, is it due to some early issues around trust?*

• *Do you select persons who are not trustworthy?*

• *Do you act in ways that alienate people?*

• *If so, what could a new Parent tell you so that you could sustain love?*

The Power of Caring

Between the ages of 30 and 60 the critical decision is whether to give parental care to others of a younger generation or whether to stagnate in self-indulgence. The successful resolution to this crisis is the development of the power of caring.

Generativity is the word for active concern for the next generation. This is not the same as having children. Some people who have children have little concern for them or for the world in which they live; they consider their children to be like attractive jewels for them to show off, or beasts of burden to be put to work doing chores. When their children grow up, move out of the home, and do not need them any more, some parents sink into depression. They suffer from identity confusion because their identity has been too closely associated with taking care of the family.

Parents like this do not think about the human species as a whole. They do not accept the importance of children in the growth of a community, or the importance of children playing, or the importance of children being with peers so that they can develop more social competence. They do not care about the next generation. Their primary concern is for themselves.

Conversely, you don't have to give birth to children to offer the care that is characteristic of generativity. Working with young people, being a good role model, or taking an active interest in the lives of young friends are all efforts at caring for the next generation. And, of course, those who care for the future of our planet—environmentalists, for example—are showing concern for the next generation.

Care is an ever-widening concern for others, not just family members. It may or may not involve physical caring out of a sense of duty. It does involve action. Truly concerned people who care are powerful people. They put their caring into action. They become involved in issues of social change and acknowledge people's rights to liberty and the pursuit of happiness. They have a healthy need to be needed, and a need to leave the world a better place for having been a part of its growing and healing.

When people are not willing to be involved in generativity by showing care for the next generation, they often find others are not concerned about them. Not caring, they become stagnant like marsh water without movement. They are increasingly less interested in others, locked into self-absorption, self-pity, or self-adoration. Frequently, their only concern is for their own satisfaction, physical health, or financial wealth.

Exercise: Escape from Self-Centeredness

Whether to stay self-centered or reach out caringly to others is a question many people need to ask themselves. The opportunity comes especially in the middle years between 30 and 60. Consider your current lifestyle and activities. Do you need to escape?

My activities that are primarily self-centered	My activities that are primarily other-centered	Activities both for myself and for others

• Is there a balance of some kind between what is primarily for you and what is primarily for others?

• If your activities seem out of balance, what do you need from a new Parent?

The Power of Wisdom

Ego integrity versus despair is the crisis that faces people after they reach their sixties. The person who has not solved this crisis is often preoccupied with self, fearful of death, and convinced that life has no meaning. Persons who have met this crisis recognize the value of their chosen lifestyles and take responsibility for what they have done, or not done, with their lives. They have ego integrity, which leads them to wisdom.

Wisdom, the happy combination of knowledge and experience, includes the awareness that life is transitory and death a certainty. So the person of integrity continually searches for the meaning to be found in later years. Long-range achievement is no longer a high priority. Short-range achievable goals take precedence. Long vacations become less important than daily pleasures. With decline in bodily strength, the wise older person is able to utilize available psychological strengths to transcend some physical frailties. A sense of impermanence pervades life. Paradoxically, there is also a sense of permanence, with the awareness that the world will endure whether or not they are there to observe it.

In the process of developing ego integrity, wise elders still pursue liberty and happiness. They often discover a new spiritual dimension to life. They have accepted their parents and stopped blaming them. They've stopped blaming themselves for being who they are. With a sense of freedom, they may review developmental crises that were not resolved earlier and change what they can change while they have time. With new wisdom comes a more detached view of life. In the final years the challenge is to meet death with faith, dignity, and a new kind of freedom.

Exercise: To Be an Elder or Be Elderly

The young find it almost impossible to comprehend what it is like to get old. Avoidance and denial are common barriers to thinking and planning for those years. When planning is done, it often is only in terms of having enough money and physical health to maintain life.

Historically, the title "elder" has been used for confidential advisors who are experienced and therefore valued for wise advice. Some cultures respect their elders and the wisdom they have accumulated; other cultures do not. Usually these are cultures that magnify the importance of money and productivity and deny or avoid other values.

Think of the various cultures (family, national, racial, etc.) you belong to. What views do they have about aging?

Do you want to fit into their views or go contrary to them?

If you want to be treated as an elder, not just someone who is elderly, what do you need to start doing now?

The Positive Value of Powerlessness

Powerlessness is generally thought to be a negative concept. But it is not always negative. Brief times of powerlessness may rejuvenate a person's body, mind, and spirit, much like a vacation does.

A period of hopelessness, about a job, a family member, or a living situation may lead to realistic appraisal and acceptance of a situation that cannot be changed. Mental and emotional energy can then be liberated for more satisfying and productive goals.

A time of self-doubt (and over-dependence) can lead to analyzing one's knowledge and value systems. This may result in a new level of intellectual and physical autonomy (as, for example, when deciding to break out of a brutalizing situation). Self-doubt could lead a person to seek education or help from others.

When guilt is experienced, the positive value may be choosing to make amends. From another perspective, a person may discover that many guilt feelings are neurotic and inappropriate. This discovery can lead to taking more initiative in life, instead of waiting for others to set the goals.

Feeling incompetent occasionally can also be useful. If social skills were not mastered between the ages of seven and twelve, or later, a person is likely to feel inferior or shy with others. Observing how other people initiate or respond in social situations can help one develop new skills that increase chances for happiness. Feeling incompetent academically is so common and widely recognized that men and women increasingly return to schools and universities. Learning something new, or getting a longed-for degree, usually increases competence and decreases feelings of inferiority.

The discomfort of re-experiencing adolescent identity confusion often activates the desire for psychotherapy or, at least, introspection about what it means to be a woman instead of a girl, or a man instead of a boy.

Occasionally feeling distant from people, or feeling cold and hateful instead of warm and loving, leads to a crisis. The crisis is a symptom of the need to choose intimacy over isolation and to actively search for people with whom this might be possible.

A change from indiscriminately taking responsibility may allow a person to become more appropriately involved with self-interest. A new experience of self-care may lead to improved health and greater enjoyment, as well as a more accurate view of reality.

Despair, the opposite of hope, is counteracted by the ego integrity that leads to wisdom. Despair can lead to awareness that continuous integration is necessary, even in the later years of life. To integrate is to make whole. It is bringing the parts together, the parts of one's personality and the parts of one's total existence.

To be healthy is to recognize holiness as well as wholeness within oneself and the rest of the world. Recognizing holiness includes recognizing the rights all people have for life, liberty and the pursuit of happiness and freedom, justice and peace.

7 Contracting for Happiness

Have you ever made a New Year's resolution such as "I'll never do that again" and, within a week, done it again?

Or made a promise "I'm going to change myself beginning now" and then delayed and delayed for months on end?

Or made a contract that "I'm going to do it even it it's hard to do" and then completed the task ahead of schedule?

If so, you know whether or not you can trust yourself to keep the resolutions, promises or contracts that you make. And if you're like most people, sometimes you do and sometimes you don't.

When people don't do what they agree to do, others lose their trust in them. Perhaps you have lost your trust in someone else, or someone may have lost trust in you. You may also doubt your own capacity to be trustworthy to yourself. The uncomfortable feeling of being unable to trust yourself may be momentary, it may be in specific situations, or it may be pervasive. Whichever it is, this self-doubt can interfere with self-reparenting. To be effective, your new Parent needs to be consistently trustworthy and supportive of your growth. You have to keep your promises to yourself to know you can trust yourself, whether those promises are little ones ("I won't cheat on my diet all day!") or big ones ("I'll stop being jealous!").

In this chapter you will learn more about being a trustworthy parent to yourself. Then you can feel less self-doubt in the pursuit of happiness. You can learn how to make agreements or contracts with yourself that you can keep. You can depend upon yourself, no matter what!

Trusting Yourself

To trust people is to be able to depend on their integrity or ability. Learning to do this is the first crisis of early childhood which, if resolved, leads to a sense of hope. Later in life it becomes clear that some people are worthy of trust because they act with integrity and some are not. Knowing whom to trust and when to trust them is liberating and assists in the pursuit of happiness.

Some people are basically trusting. They tend to trust everybody, including themselves. Others are suspicious or even despairing and trust nobody, including themselves. Others, usually with low self-esteem and a sense of inadequacy, do not trust themselves, although they may expect others to be trustworthy. People who only trust themselves believe other people are not dependable or capable enough.

These attitudes about trust may exist in varying degrees or at varying levels of intensity. For example, persons who are basically trusting may actually exaggerate their own and other people's commitments and capacities. They may see the entire world through rose-colored glasses and ignore problems that really exist. A different pattern is noticeable in persons who are always helping others. They may trust only themselves, refusing to believe that other people are competent and can usually direct their own lives.

People are fortunate if they have had other people in their lives whom they could depend upon and trust. Now, however, the focus is on being a trusting, responsible, motivating, and committed parent to yourself.

Contracting for success and knowing that success is possible requires an awareness of your own attitudes about trusting—an awareness of promises that have been kept and promises that have been broken— especially the promises made to yourself.

Making plans

Exercise: Promises, Promises

During your life you have probably made many promises to yourself that you may or may not have kept. The ways you kept or did not keep your promises reflect some of your strengths or weaknesses.

Promises I made to myself	How I managed to keep them	Excuses I used for breaking them	Excuses were valid or not valid

The excuses you used for breaking your promises may have been valid if the promises were unrealistic because the goals were not achievable, no matter what.

The excuses you used that were invalid reflect the need for a firmer new Parent, perhaps a tough Parent instead of a permissive one.

Write what you think about the possibility of needing a firm new Parent who will insist on your keeping your promises to yourself.

Contracting Theory

Being trustworthy to yourself so that you are able to give up habits that interfere with your happiness is a natural, healthy way to self-care. It will lead you to success in many areas of your life. Perhaps you want to be more successful in the financial part of your life, or your sex life, or your family life, or in your education or some other area. If so, the area you are dissatisfied with may need a radical change or improvement. In addition, the positive changes you have already made may need to be reinforced so that they remain a strong, consistent part of you. Deliberate changes usually are based on contracts.

A *contract* is an agreement to do something about something, such as taking time out for a vacation or completing a project by a certain date or solving a problem that is creating too much physical or emotional stress.

Contracts are part of everyone's daily life. They can be legalized or not. Some contracts, such as marriage contracts or employment contracts, are legal contracts and breaking them often requires the services of an attorney. Other contracts, such as completing a specific curriculum at school, or making regular deposits to a savings account, or engaging in an exercise program, are not regulated by law. Yet, the successful completion of these kinds of contracts usually increases a person's self-esteem. Completion also raises motivation and increases strength to make more contracts that will lead to further satisfaction.

Successful contracts made with yourself need to be cooperative ventures. At least two parts of the personality need to agree that a change is desirable. The inner Child needs to be aware of wanting something that will lead to success and happinesss. The logical Adult part of the personality needs to agree and (urged by the Child) to figure out if what is wanted is possible to obtain. Some things are impossible. The world won't fit on a silver platter regardless of how hard a person might want it that way.

Exercise: A Tentative Plan

The successful achievement of a goal usually requires a plan of action and a decision to start. Before that time, a tentative plan is often useful.

What I want is

The resources I already have are

My first or next step would be

I could take that step on

Then I would

I would evaluate the plan in process by

My new-Parent response to this tentative plan might be

Basic Requirements

After deciding what would enhance life and establishing a specific goal, a plan is needed. Before the plan is made, there are basic requirements to be met. These requirements include an awareness of the time available, the energy to be expended, and the level of motivation needed.

One of the most important requirements for reaching a goal is the capacity to use time effectively. People can use their time in the pursuit or enjoyment of success, or can misuse it so that most plans they make are doomed to fail.

Restructuring the use of time is sometimes hard because of the choices involved. Choice is often difficult. People who already fill their time in enjoyable and productive ways may not want to give up any current activities even for more enjoyment and productivity. Others who overplan and overschedule themselves fill their time in less enjoyable and less productive ways. Like jugglers who are able to keep many balls in the air at once until there are one too many balls, persons who overschedule usually feel driven or enslaved instead of liberated, happy, and successful.

Nonplanners of time represent a different type of person. Whether active or passive in behavior, these people prefer things to just happen. Some feel critical or resentful of others who plan how they are going to use their time. Others feel helpless when they compare themselves to those who use time productively. Unwilling to take charge of their own use of time, they passively resist changing themselves or responding to others who would encourage change.

Change requires the expenditure of energy. Since everyone works with limited energy, the question "What must I do to reach my goal?" may seem overwhelming because of the energy needed during the pursuit.

When that seems to be the case, ask the questions: "How am I allowing my energy to be blocked?" "How am I allowing my energy to be drained off so I have little left to reach my goal?" "How am I allowing my anxiety or fear of success or failure to interfere with my planning for success?"

Another basic requirement before establishing a firm plan is the motivation to make the plan work or to revise it so that it will work. When people are motivated, they are stimulated to action. Self-motivation is based on the belief that the pursuit or achievement of a particular goal will give life more value. Motivation is related to values. If people value friendship, they find life to be meaningful when they are with friends. Thus, they structure their time and energy because of what they value. They know what they want, and they know what they need to do.

Goal-Setting for Success

Setting goals that will lead to more success is a major challenge in self-reparenting. Many people set goals that cannot be met because they involve trying to make someone else change. If the other person wants to change, well and good. If not, failure is inevitable.

The most successful goals are those that involve changing oneself. In self change, specific goals need to be established, then evaluated to see if they are practical and achievable. If not practical and achievable, the goals must be revised until they meet these criteria. It is also important that progress can be measured. If, for example, someone wants to cut down on smoking, it is necessary to state the goal in numbers: "I want to go from 40 cigarettes a day to ten." If someone wants to improve the world, it is necessary to decide in what specific way and also to evaluate the possibility of success.

When goals are overly optimistic, not realistic and not revised (the fate of many New Year's resolutions), they are not achieved. When resolutions are not kept and goals are not met, old decisions about being inadequate or not being able to trust oneself are likely to be recycled. Then they are replayed like a scratched 78-rpm record that you listen to because it's familiar in spite of your discomfort.

Goals with the potential of success are those that are reasonable and practical and within people's power to achieve. When the goals are achieved, the taste of success is sweet and happiness results. Successful goals depend on sound plans as well as sufficient motivation to initiate action.

Some people know their goals, and usually know exactly what they want. Others are not so sure what they want. They just know they want to be happy. Pinpointing the area of life that is not satisfying often leads to the ability to focus on specific plans for improvement. If you are not clear about what you want, refer to Chapter 2 to the diagram on "Life Areas of Satisfaction" (page 25) and select one area that you think you need to change from a minus to a plus quality.

Organizing time

Exercise: Awareness of Requirements

Think of a project you would like to undertake, then assess it in terms of the time, energy, and motivation you will need to complete it.

The number of hours (per day, week or month) that would be needed are approximately _____ .

I have that time available, or I could have, by restructuring my use of time. _____ (If no, then select a different project.)

yes or no

Energy that would be required is _____ for me.

possible or imposible
If impossible, select a different project.

My level of motivation to start and complete the project is _____ . (If low, then select another project.)

low or high

With each goal you establish continue to ask yourself about the requirements of time, energy, and motivation.

Exercise: Realistic and Measurable Contracts

To be successful, contracts must be clear, precise, and direct. They also need to be based on realistic and practical goals.

List a number of things you would like to have or places you would like to go or ways in which you would like to change. Then evaluate.

What I want	Is it realistic to pursue?	How could I measure my progress?

Be aware that what you want may not be what your parents of the past want you to have. If that is the case, deliberately increase your motivation.

Changing Habits for Success

Habits are learned patterns of behavior and involve consistent ways of thinking, feeling, and acting. Some habits are positive and contribute to success, some are negative and lead to a sense of failure. They often start in childhood and, like addictions, are difficult to give up. Making effective contracts to change unwanted habits, and trusting yourself to keep your contracts, leads to success, even happiness.

Habits that do not lead to success can be changed for those that do. For example, some people escape from reality or from other people by watching too much television. It becomes a habit that may be given up by becoming more involved in study or sports or hobbies of some kind. Carelessness about exercise and eating, about personal hygiene and appearance, may be replaced by new habits that enhance health and good looks.

Habits can be changed in many ways. Sometimes they are changed by external pressure or encouragement from others. Sometimes they change because of internal pressure or encouragement from oneself. When the external pressure "You should change, and you can do it" is congruent with the internal pressure "I want to change, and I am going to do it", people experience new energy and the capacity to trust themselves with a plan for action.

Negative habits are like chains. One link often leads to another. A workaholic, after a long hard day, may by habit work even longer, or by habit stop at the local bar for a few drinks on the way home, or by habit collapse in front of the TV emotionally withdrawn from family or friends. The overworking behavior is often linked to self-pity or grandiose expectations and may be like an addiction. The new Parent may need to insist on the Adult's taking more time to relax or more vacations to break up the self-destructive habit.

Exercise: Habits to Keep or Change

You already know many of your habits, such as the processes you go through when you wake up in the morning or before you go to bed at night.

This particular exercise is to increase your awareness of how these contribute to or interfere with your happiness.

Make a list of habitual ways you act, think, or feel when at home, at work, and in social situations.

Habitual patterns	I like this about me because	I need to change this because

Designing a Specific Goal

After determining the general area of life where change is wanted, the next step is to focus on specifics. For example, persons who are dissatisfied with their educational backgrounds may need to clarify what they want instead. Do they wish they had studied in a different field or gone to a different school or applied themselves more seriously to the courses they took? They need to decide on specific goals that, if achieved, would make up for what they consider to be deficits in their education.

As another example, persons who are dissatisfied with their physical health may need to be very clear on what they want instead. Do they want to lose weight or gain weight? If so, how many pounds? They will need to analyze themselves to determine whether they are motivated enough to keep their own commitments to some form of self-care such as dieting or exercising.

If you are dissatisfied with your family life or social life or sexual life, what exactly do you want instead? What goal would enhance life and have the potential for success? It is not enough to want to be happier. Happiness can be in the planning. It can be during the pursuit. It can come with the achievement.

If, time after time, people make promises to themselves and then break them, it means the promises have been built on grandiose expectations or insufficient commitment, not reality. Specific goals can only be reached if the expectations are reasonable and meet some of the needs and wants of the inner Child.

Exercise: What Do I Want to Enhance My Life?

Review the exercises in Chapter 5 (pages 120-121) on the needs and wants of your inner Child. Start with some small goals that you could achieve if you decided to exert the time and energy. Be specific.

Things I want or need that would enhance my life	What an encouraging new Parent would say about what I want

Exercise: What Do I Need to Do?

Consider the areas in your life that you would like to change. Then focus your attention on a specific change and discover whether you are really committed to your goal.

Specific goal I want to achieve:

What I need to do to reach this goal:

What else I need to do to reach this goal:

I would restructure my time by:

I would focus my energy by:

My motivation to reach this goal is:

Therefore, I conclude:

Letting Go of Fear

Some people experience irrational fears that interfere with the making of contracts. Clear and direct techniques have been developed to solve these problems by systematically desensitizing a person until the fear is radically reduced or, in many cases, completely eliminated. For example, uncontrollable fear of dogs or snakes or people, of school exams or social situations, of heights, of closed places, of being alone, of going crazy, can be cured when people become desensitized.

The first step in desensitization is deep muscle relaxation in a comfortable, safe situation. Then a person is asked to visualize a very mild form of that which is feared. In this way the anxiety level is also very mild. Over successive days, the visualization technique can become stronger and more realistic. If anxiety gets too high, the process is stopped until the person becomes internally quiet again. Then the desensitization process is continued. An effective new inner Parent will protect the inner Child and allow only as much as can comfortably be integrated.

For example, if a person is very afraid to leave the house, the first step is relaxation, then visualization of going to the door. The next day, after relaxation the visualization might be expanded to include turning the doorknob or opening the door but not going any farther. In time, the visualizations lead to actions so that the person actually goes to the door and opens it. With patience and time the fear that has so restricted life and liberty is overcome. A celebration is in order!

Exercise: Desensitizing Your Fears

Becoming less sensitive can occur because of a new decision, or it may be a gradual process. Either way, it can liberate you to live more fully.

List those things you are sensitive about (such as being evaluated or criticized) or objects or situations you actually fear (such as being alone on a dark night or when physically ill).

Fears I have	How the fear affects me	How life would be different if I weren't afraid

Now select one of your fears and design a plan for desensitization. Let your encouraging, loving new Parent help you plan, so that putting the plan in action will not be too threatening or too hard for you.

One of my fears is:

What I need to do about it is:

The time and place to begin is:

Helpful messages I need from my new inner Parent are:

How I plan to celebrate is:

The Cost of Change

After people establish a particular goal and develop a workable plan to reach it, their next step is determining the cost during the pursuit and the cost when the goal is reached. There is always a cost. Sometimes the cost is financial as, for example, when you pay a tuition fee for further study. Sometimes the cost is physical, as when you get less sleep while working and going to school concurrently. Sometimes the cost is emotional, such as feeling conflict because a spouse is critical of the time, energy, and money spent by the one who wishes to study. In any case, when a goal is chosen and the requirements for reaching the goal are clear, there is a cost and it must be reckoned with. Whatever the cost, it is usually experienced as stress.

Many people are not willing to pay the cost. They find they are not willing to do what is needed for whatever reason. Then they need to revise their goals or choose a different goal in which they have a higher level of motivation. They need to decide whether they want to use the power of the will. They need to decide whether they will continue to procrastinate or to let fear and self-doubt rule their lives. They need to know the potential cost and, if tolerable, set out courageously with a sense of trust.

Exercise: What Am I Willing to Do?

You know what you want that would enhance your life and what you need to do to get it. Now the question is what are you willing to do. Are you willing to pay the cost?

One goal I want to reach is:

Briefly, what I need to do to reach it is:

What I am willing to do is:

The costs of pursuing this goal are likely to be:

The costs of not pursuing this goal are likely to be:

Therefore, I am _____ *to pursue this goal.*
                                 willing or not willing

Success Shows

Success is not something that is easily hidden. It shows in many ways. Sometimes it can be seen in someone's improved health—in the new sparkle in their eyes or the bounce in the way they walk. Sometimes it shows in a changed lifestyle, in the better use of time and the enjoyment of both work and play. Sometimes it shows in the use of money, finally spending it wisely instead of with credit-card impulsiveness or miser-like hoarding. Sometimes success shows in changed relationships with others. Destructive relationships may be discarded and life-enhancing relationships may be developed and cherished. Success shows in any area of life when goals to improve that part of life are established and achieved.

It is important to be clear how you will know when you reach your goal. If you are going for a university degree, it will show when you get your diploma. If you are going for a new job, your success will show when you get it. If your goal is to lose weight, it will show when you get on the scales or buy a smaller size of clothing. Create signposts of success for that you recognize your goals when you reach them.

Some people worry about being successful because they believe that others will be jealous of their success. That may be true. Others may in fact become jealous or resentful or angry. Accepting that as a possibility, not a probability, can be liberating. Dwelling on it can be enslaving and can interfere with the successful pursuit of happiness.

Exercise: How Will My Success Show?

You will know when you succeed in reaching your goal because it will affect your life in some way. Others may also know, if your success affects them, or if it is observable in some way. How might it go for you?

Goals I am going for	How I'll experience my success	How my success might show to others

Now check out the new Parent you have been developing and design a motivating Parent statement that will fit your goals for the future and the success you are planning for:

The Possibility of Sabotage

Achieving a goal is often delayed or prevented by sabotage. In the self-reparenting process, sabotage is replaying the old parental messages or the negative feelings and behaviors of childhood. These obstructions to the procedure interfere with success and sometimes lead to failure.

Another way to failure instead of success is the gradual undermining of something. Like water that slowly wears away a foundation of a building or like a house built on sand, the unwillingness to remain consistently firm and loving to yourself erodes your freedom and establishes barriers that are hard to overcome in the pursuit of happiness.

Refusing to be a trustworthy Parent to yourself is the easiest way to undermine potential success. Therefore, it is necessary to know in what areas of life you can trust yourself and in what areas you are not trustworthy. Do you keep your promises to yourself or sabotage your goals as you work to achieve them?

Some goals are reasonable; some are not

Exercise: How Might I Fail?

People choose unique ways of sabotaging or undermining the goals they establish. They may surround themselves with negative people, repeat negative messages to themselves, procrastinate indefinitely, or act in numerous ways that contribute to failure instead of success.

Knowing your potential for sabotaging your own goals will help you fight against these tendencies.

Goals I hope to reach	How I could sabotage myself	What I could do instead

When Others Judge

Knowing who you are, as well as how you respond to other people, especially if they are critical, is a very important problem in establishing contracts for success.

Some people set goals that are much lower than their potential. They may be afraid that others will be jealous or will avoid them if they succeed. They may think it is disloyal to be more successful than others in their family. They may have decided in childhood that they could never succeed, regardless of how hard they tried. They may have given up trying to get affirmation or approval.

Many people are deeply afraid of being criticized, usually because of experiences in childhood. Even when they become competent adults, some still imagine criticism will turn into brutality, as it once did. Or they imagine a criticism is a threat that implies somebody will withdraw their love.

In any case, they see others as both judge and jury whether the others are capable in these roles or not. They tend to see themselves as misunderstood victims. Solving this problem requires analyzing potential prejudices of others to decide when it is safe to tell and when it is wiser to be silent.

Exercise: How Will Others Respond?

Most people need some form of help from other people when they are in the process of changing. All too often they tell about a potential change to someone who will criticize or ridicule them or their goals.

People I might tell	Their probable response	The response would help or hinder	Therefore, I will or won't tell

When contracting, it is very effective to tell people who will show parental encouragement and give logical feedback about your goals.

Trust your new Parent to advise you on who to tell.

Exercise: A First-Aid Kit for Emergencies

It is not unusual for people to suddenly feel angry or confused or depressed while making changes and paying the costs of changing.

If this occurs, it is useful to have the equivalent of a fantasy first-aid kit. Perhaps it would be permission to go to a movie or have a leisurely dinner or long bubble bath or listen to favorite music or read a favorite book or visit an art gallery or phone a friend. Some people put actual objects they enjoy or pictures of friends they love into a box labeled "First Aid for the Blues." What might help you in an emergency?

• Sit down and relax quietly.

• Let yourself drift into a peaceful scene.

• Reflect on what might be useful when you are tense, worried, anxious, or hurt.

• Consider putting what might be useful into your first-aid kit.

The Motivating Parent

To carry out the program of self-reparenting, people need motivation. Sick people may visit physicians because they are motivated to get well. Hungry people may stop at a restaurant because they are motivated to eat. Unhappy people may visit psychotherapists because they are motivated to regain mental health. Uninformed people may go to school because they are motivated to learn more.

People want to change and improve themselves for a variety of reasons. The stronger their motivation, the likelier they are to set goals for desired change. They will restructure their time to plan for the effective use of their energies.

Each contract made and successfully completed requires careful goal setting, plus an evaluation of costs and ways to assess progress. Using a new Parent who is trustworthy and encouraging makes contracting easier to do and a joy to complete. Healthy parents motivate people to be happy.

8 Celebrating Your Happiness

Did you ever want to have a celebration party, or go to one and not know how to behave?

Did you ever plan a celebration and have it turn out wrong or boring or miserable?

Do you ever fantasize about having a wonderful celebration with all your friends?

Or do you fantasize that a celebration wouldn't be fun and nobody would want to come anyway?

When you think of the future, do you look forward to celebrating your successes, or do you avoid thinking about your potential successes or your opportunities for success and happiness?

These questions are all concerned with time, past and future. However, *now* is the time you are living. Now is influenced by the positive and negative experiences of the past and, in turn, will affect what happens in your future. You can decide to live now with courage and zest, expressing your life energy in celebration, or you can reinforce negative experiences and feelings of the past. You can, if you choose, forgive the parents of your past who were not perfect and forgive yourself for being as human as they were. You can enjoy happiness now. You can celebrate who you are, what you have done with your life so far and what you intend to do in the future. The right to happiness is yours.

Celebrating Life

Children don't like to be mistreated by their parents. Parents, being people, don't like being mistreated either. Your new Parent is still very new. Treat it with courtesy and respect and with acceptance and love and you will be treated the same. Your life will be richer, your liberty more extensive, your success and happiness greater.

Each part of you, as you continue to become more integrated and whole, will need positive reinforcement. You will need opportunities for joy and laughter and intellectual challenges that will stretch your mind. You will need friends who are fun and thoughtful and nourishing. Sometimes you will celebrate with them and sometimes alone.

Although life contains inevitable suffering, it can also be like a movable feast where each day you discover something large or small that calls for celebration. The causes are innumerable: sunrises and sunsets, moonlight and stars, the first spring flowers or first fall of snow, the call of the wild geese, the sound of the surf, the smell of the prairie, the crackle of a fire on the hearth, the touch of soft wind on the skin, the cool taste of melon in your mouth. These sensory causes cost little—only awareness and the decision to enjoy.

Then there are other causes for celebration that include more than the senses: the snap of a fish on the line, the welcoming bark of a dog, the loving smile from a child, the unexpected letter from a friend. More causes may be finding something important that was lost or finding something important that you never quite had—like finding yourself and your own unique ways to happiness.

The form of celebration may be brief and cost nothing, like hugging yourself or phoning a friend. It may be experienced as a high moment of delight or as a short prayer of relief and thanksgiving. If you have a party or if you take a vacation or if you take a sabbatical from work to study where and what you want to study, your celebration may be longer.

Whatever the causes or form of your celebrations, time and space will be somewhat irrelevant when they occur. The past and future will be felt in the present. Therefore, if you consider your life and whatever liberty you have to be like a movable feast, the moments of happiness will increase and be more intense. You will recognize that to succeed in your pursuit of happiness is always your right.

Rights and Rites

In the English language, the words *rights* and *rites* are pronounced the same, yet have different spellings and very different meanings. *Right* is used in many ways to refer to action, direction, accuracy, and so forth. In this book your right to happiness refers both to birthright and to privilege. Because you were born, you have a right to happiness.

The work *rite* is most often used for some kind of significant ceremony. All cultures have rites regarding birth, marriage, and death. Another kind of rite occurs when a king or president or religious leader takes office. The solemnity of some rites, such as First Communion or Bar Mitzvah, is intended to demonstrate their importance. Yet not all rites are solemn. Some, like weddings, are joyful. Rites can touch the wellsprings of the heart and release joy and thanksgiving. When there is an outpouring of positive feeling, it is energizing. There is a new zest for life.

Exercise: Energy and the Zest for Life

The zest for life is a positive energy that enhances our days and leads us to enjoy life as it is or to strive for something more.

For this exercise, relax for a moment, take a few slow breaths, and let yourself re-experience times when you felt high positive energy and the zest for life. Then consider what was involved and why you think you felt that way.

Situations when I felt high positive energy	Why I felt that way	What I did with my energy

Now consider the times when your energy was low or negative and life did not seem worth living.

Situations when I felt low energy or very negative	Why I felt that way	What I did with my energy

Celebration Takes Many Forms

Birthdays, anniversaries, graduations, job advancement, or the birth of a child are only a few of the causes for celebration. They are celebrated in many ways—with cake and candles, presents, and games, cocktail parties, invitations, vacations, special music, gifts, favored foods, places or activities.

Celebrations may be highly organized, like a parade with bands playing, groups marching, and flags waving to honor a national holiday. Or, more spontaneous, they may take the form of a beer party for a few people after a sports event. They may involve thousands of people, as when peace is declared after a long war, or two people, celebrating a promotion. In every case, the merrymaking proclaims something important has happened and that people have the right to be happy.

People design some celebrations according to cultural norms. One person's retirement party may include the traditional presentation of a gold watch and a formal dinner dance. Another's may involve a picnic with balloons, music, and light-hearted dancing on the beach.

Sometimes, in order to celebrate, it is necessary to change habitual ways of responding to friends, colleagues, and famly members. Occasionally it may seem wise to break off relationships or to spend less time with critical or depressing people who may stand in the way of change and growth. Less time with unhappy people may allow you to develop new relationships that are friendly, growth-enhancing, responsible, and conducive to happiness.

Exercise: How Do I Celebrate? Let Me Count the Ways

One way to evaluate yourself and your opportunities for enjoyment is to think in terms of your own "life, liberty and pursuit of happiness."

In this exercise, become aware of what you do celebrate and what you don't. Your life (your good health)? Your liberty (an unexpected day off from work)? Your pursuit of happiness (enjoying new friends)?

Some of the ways I currently celebrate my life are:

Some of the ways I currently celebrate my liberty are:

Some of the ways I currently celebrate my pursuit of happiness are:

Consider your responses. Are you missing out on some chances for joyful celebration?

• If so, what specific advice would an ideal new Parent give you?

Instead of Celebrating

Instead of celebrating, many successful people hide their successes. They refuse to celebrate and feel happy, frequently using one of the following excuses: their success is not really important and they may be ridiculed or ignored; their success will make someone jealous, and a friendship or work relation may be harmed; they will be expected to perform still another task, and to perform it even more successfully; they are angry at someone or at a situation or even angry at the world; they fear it might take too much time away from their pursuit of other goals; they feel they do not deserve recognition and joy, either because they have failed in some other way or because "anything good that happens is just luck."

Regardless of which excuse a person may use, avoiding celebration is a way of denying the potential excitement of living. The feelings of happiness that well up from a person's inner core deserve recognition.

Hoorah for you

Exercise: The Anti-Enjoyment Excuses

Everyone's life has some moments of happiness. Celebrating them increases the positive effect if people are willing to do so.

Do you use anti-enjoyment excuses to yourself or others to restrict your celebrations? "It's not really important," "Nobody cares," "If I let someone know, I'll be expected to do more," "They'll be jealous if they know," "I don't have time," "It was just luck. I don't deserve the credit." Fill in the chart and assess your willingness to celebrate.

Celebrations I have initiated	Celebrations I could have initiated and didn't	Excuses I used for not celebrating

• *For a few minutes visualize yourself going through life with very few celebrations.*

• *Now visualize yourself having many.*

• *What is your choice, and what are you going to do about your choice?*

Losing the Energy to Celebrate

People often use excuses to avoid celebrations because they have experienced a loss of energy. They feel debilitated, so they do not anticipate enjoyment. It is important to see that enjoying celebrations is a choice. Sometimes not enjoying them is normal. For example, when people are shocked by bad news, or are seriously ill, celebrations are of low priority. People need to conserve energy to cope with stress they are experiencing. At other times, they may feel more energized if they look around and see how much there is in life to feel good about.

Some people, even when things are going well, are not energized enough to celebrate. Energy for celebrating is especially low in three situations: first, when traditions are too restrictive and act like a dam; second, when not taking enough time for oneself, or saying yes to too many demands, or trying to be perfect, drains off too much energy; third, when anxiety is so high the energy has difficulty getting expressed.

In many families and cultures there are laws or customs that spell out the details of celebrations. Like dams, laws may restrict the free flow of energy until pressure builds up and a break occurs. People who refuse to celebrate often build up pressure and, like dams, may also break down. They can choose not to. They can choose to change some of the restrictive customs. Or, if the customs can't be changed, they can change their responses to them. Instead of feeling bound, their energy can flow freely. A good new Parent would encourage this.

The second way people experience energy loss is when they are continually drained by the demands they put upon themselves or accept from others. They "can't say no;" instead they habitually put others first, try to please everyone, and do more than their share of work. These people are likely to prepare too hard for a celebration, becoming so tired they don't enjoy it; or don't get enough rest afterward and, having as usual too many obligations the next day, feel drained.

They don't have to do this. They can choose to say "no" to some demands made on them. They can work easy instead of hard. They can take more time to enjoy life before feeling drained . They can be assertive on behalf of themselves, and a good new Parent would also encourage this.

The third way to experience energy loss is by worrying. If every event causes anxiety and doubt, there won't be enough energy left to enjoy yourself. Parties, in particular, seem to bring out high levels of stress and anxiety in many people. Some people worry about their appearance, or the refreshments, or what the neighbors might say, or who to invite. Worrying depletes energy. This is not necessary.

People can choose. They can remind themselves that nothing has to be perfect. Joy is not based on perfection. It is based on being open to the wonders of the universe, and a good Parent will encourage this openness.

Exercise: Energizing Yourself

In this exercise, think about your river of energy and its flow. Be aware of how you can release your energy so it isn't blocked or drained off or restricted.

Customs or traditions that block my energy	What I could do about them	What I'm willing to do about each one

People, tasks or situations that take too much energy	What I could do about each one	What I am willing to do about each one

Anxieties and worries that interfere with free-flowing energy	What I need to do about each one	What I'm willing to do about each one

As you reflect on the above, how about planning a little celebration for yourself because you are releasing your energy to pursue happiness and to celebrate it.

Deciding to Forgive

The ability to think clearly and act rationally as well as lovingly is immediately increased when people decide to forgive their parents and others. The energy to celebrate life is also increased when people let go of resentment and anger and forgive themselves for what they have done in the past. Forgiveness is one of the most important parts of self-reparenting and involves redecision.

All young people make decisions about themselves, about other people and about how the world is or should be. Many people do not alter their original decisions. They cling to them in spite of evidence that shows the decisions to be faulty or circumstances to have changed.

If they become aware of their faulty decisions, they can change them—sometimes by desensitization techniques, sometimes by re-education, sometimes by redecisions.

Redecision is often involved in problems regarding parents, a common issue brought to therapists. One of the most effective ways to increase your energy for continuing growth is to decide to forgive your parents and parent figures who were less than perfect. It is most empowering when forgiveness is both intellectual and emotional. The resulting release of tension frees energy. It is as if the slate is wiped clean, the day is new and fresh without the pollutions of the past. Forgiveness is the granting of pardon without holding resentment. It is not just saying "I forgive you." It is more than that. It is giving up resentment, anger, hate, and even self-righteousness. It is forgiving the humanness of others as well as your own humanness. It is recognizing that your parents were influenced by their parents and culture, even as you were. Forgiveness often involves regret that your life, and theirs, were not different. Yet this step is necessary to achieve happiness.

There are many ways to go about the process of forgiving one's parents. Some people use meditation to quiet themselves and let go of resentment. Some pray for the strength to forgive. In either case, they often experience a change in attitude, with more acceptance of their parents. Different types of people may use an intellectual approach and begin to recognize that their parents were enslaved just as they were, and that to continue finding fault only leads to greater unhappiness. Another common way is replaying, with emotion, early childhood scenes, then replaying them with a different sequence or ending.

Exercise: Forgiving Your Parents

This exercise is not for everyone. Some readers may not need to forgive their parents for not being perfect because they have already done so. However, if any resentment remains, this will help. Read the directions several times, then begin.

- *Pick a quiet time when other people are not around. Place two chairs facing each other and sit in one.*

- *Relax, take a few deep breaths, and visualize one or both of your parents sitting opposite you.*

- *Start a conversation with one or both by explaining how you have stayed resentful for so long. Then listen to what they say. If you feel comfortable doing so, move to the other chair and role-play your parents speaking to you.*

- *Continue the dialogue and let your feelings emerge (perhaps grief, or anger). Don't be afraid of your feelings; they belong to you and are under your control.*

- *As you continue the dialogue, you may experience the pain in your parents' lives that influenced them to be the way they were. If so, let yourself feel compassion. Then let your compassion lead to forgiveness.*

- *Now write a short note to them, whether they are alive or dead. In the note explain the value of forgiveness and how it releases you.*

Exercise: Forgiving Yourself

Any celebration you have may turn out superficial or even dismal if you have not forgiven yourself. Many people find it all too easy to remember their own errors of judgment, and their own improprieties.

• If you have some of this unfinished business, think of something you are ashamed of. Then ask yourself:

Have I made amends as best I could? If not, why not?

If so, why am I unwilling to forgive myself?

How would my life be different if I did?

• Now start an inner dialogue with your encouraging new Parent and listen to the advice.

• Stop hanging onto the misery of the past.

• Hold out your hands in front of you and shake them hard. Experience letting go.

• Write yourself a letter telling yourself it is finished, that you forgive yourself and that you are going to stop being so critical of yourself and get on with life and happiness.

Laughter: The Medicine That Heals

Forgiving oneself and others is curative medicine and cause for celebration. So is laughter, which is part of many celebrations. Healthy laughter activates the chemistry for the will to live. It often reflects joy and insight, attracts friends and lovers, breaks tension in uncomfortable social situations and seemingly increases the capacity to fight against disease. By expanding the chest and increasing respiration, laughter relaxes the body and helps stimulate the balance called health. Laughter also releases the capacity to enjoy other people, because the universal ability to play, to create, and to have fun is liberating.

One of the signs of mental health is the capacity to laugh at yourself. A healthy laugh is not a laugh of ridicule. It can be a laugh of insight when the cause or the solution to a problem is suddenly clear. It can be like the laugh of pleased parents who are enjoying the first steps of a child. It can be a laugh of delight between friends or an invitation between lovers.

What people laugh at differs from century to century, from culture to culture, and even from one stage of life to another. And part of being human is accepting the fact that what is funny to one person is often not funny to another. Listen to a six-year-old learning to tell riddles (or the six-year-old in the grown-up) then to a teenager telling sexual jokes, and observe the difference. Yet laughter is contagious, and healthy laughter celebrates in some way the right to happiness.

Do you remember a time when you watched a funny movie or read a funny story? Do you remember how good your body felt after a deep laugh? Do you remember how clearly you experienced yourself and the rest of the world at that time?

These experiences are easy to reproduce. You can choose to laugh. Even if nothing is funny you can laugh and your body will feel more relaxed. You can laugh and you will feel less emotional tension. You can laugh at all the absurdities of life—even at yourself.

Exercise: Laugh and the World Laughs with You

Experiment with some new ways to get people to laugh with you—just for fun.

Get a humorous book, go to a public place like a park or airport and start reading it and laughing. Experiment with a chuckle or a guffaw or a giggle. See what happens with the people around you.

Phone a friend and talk about something funny that's happened to you. Maybe your friend will have a humorous incident for you.

Get a small group together and do a chuck-a-belly fun exercise. In this, people lie down in a line and put their heads on the stomachs of the next person. Laughter starts at one end of the line a builds up. Tension is reduced and a sense of community is experienced.

Have a party, dress up in funny clothes, like a come-as-you-aren't party, get a funny game going or sing some funny songs, tell some limericks. Play charades. Laugh, enjoy and celebrate. Your new Parent is on your side.

Exercise: Creating a Bumper Sticker: Just for Laughs

In many places in the world it is customary to put stickers on car bumpers. These stickers usually have some kind of slogan or saying. They may show a political preference, reflect an envied travel destination, advertise a skill or a product, or invite others to think or to laugh.

In this exercise, to reinforce your positive gains, design several fantasy bumper stickers, such as "From Culpable to Capable" or "Born to Win and Now I Know It" or "Smile and the World Smiles With You" or "Happiness Is My Right." If you're feeling playful, try "Honk If Your're Happy."

Next, print your slogans on strips of paper about four inches wide and two feet long and put them on your car or give them to friends for their cars.

Laugh and be happy

A Message from a Nurturing Parent

Along with laughing and celebrating please love yourself and take care of yourself. You will probably outlive your parents and other parent figures. You may outlive or precede in death your close friends whom you parent and who parent you. The boldness of your youth may mellow like fine wine, your values may change, your lifestyle alter. Loss, loneliness and sorrow are possible at any time, and that's the bad news.

The good news is that joy and laughter and experiencing the wholeness of life while feeling part of all creation is also possible. You can choose. It's not too late.

As you choose, please choose happiness on an hour-to-hour, day-by-day basis along with your plans for future happiness. Happiness is often a peak experience, a high point. It's worth the struggle. Even though you are sometimes unhappy, remember you can survive and courageously pursue happiness again and again.

A Final Word

Last, but not least, how about giving a party for your new Parent! Or how about giving two parties—one for your new Parent *and* one that your new Parent gives for you!

Here is a sample invitation to the celebration you could have to announce that you have succeeded in your action-based program for happiness.

You Are Invited

to share a celebration with me

date _____

time _____

place _____

I hope you can come.
Your presence will enhance my life.

_____
(name)

R.S.V.P.

P.S. I enjoy parties, and if you invite me, I might be able to come. However, even if I don't, I will be glad to know of your successful pursuit of happiness.

P.P.S. If you ever want to come to a program on this subject, or tell me about the effect of this book on your life, please write to me at P.O. Box 356, Lafayette, CA 94549. Meanwhile, take care!

Selected Bibliography

Beck, Aaron T., M.D. *COGNITIVE THERAPY AND THE EMOTIONAL DISORDERS*. New York: New American Library, 1976.

Benson, Herbert, M.D. with Klipper, Miriam Z. *THE RELAXATION RESPONSE*. New York: William Morrow and Company, Inc., 1975.

Bowlby, John. *ATTACHMENT AND LOSS, VOL. I*. New York: Basic Books, 1969.

Bowlby, John. *ATTACHMENT AND LOSS, VOL. II. SEPARATION ANXIETY AND ANGER*. New York: Basic Books, 1973.

Brown, Barbara B. *SUPERMIND: THE ULTIMATE ENERGY*. New York: Harper & Row, 1980.

Burns, David D., M.D. *FEELING GOOD*. New York: New American Library, 1980.

Cousins, Norman. "Anatomy of an Illness (as perceived by the patient)." *NEW ENGLAND JOURNAL OF MEDICINE*, 1976, 19458-19463.

Donaldson, M. *CHILDREN'S MINDS*. New York: Norton, 1979.

Duska, Ronald and Whelan, Mariellen. *MORAL DEVELOPMENT: A GUIDE TO PIAGET AND KOHLBERG*. New York: Paulist Press, 1975.

Elias, Norbert. *THE CIVILIZING PROCESS: THE DEVELOPMENT OF MANNERS* (Edmund Jephcott, trans.). New York: Urizen Books, 1978.

Ellenberger, Henri. *THE DISCOVERY OF THE UNCONSCIOUS: THE HISTORY AND EVOLUTION OF DYNAMIC PSYCHIATRY*. New York: Basic Books, 1970.

Erikson, Erik. *CHILDHOOD AND SOCIETY* (2nd ed.). New York: W.W. Norton, 1963.

Erikson, Erik. "Identity and the Life Cycle." *PSYCHOLOGICAL ISSUES*, 1, 1958, monograph 1.

Evans, R.E. *DIALOGUE WITH ERIK ERIKSON*. New York: Harper & Row, 1967.

Fielding, Elizabeth R. "Cultural Scripting and Aging." *TRANSACTIONAL ANALYSIS JOURNAL*, Vol. 14, No. 1, January 1984.

Fiore, Neil A. *THE ROAD BACK TO HEALTH*. New York: Bantam Books, 1984.

Fraiberg, Selma. *THE MAGIC YEARS*. New York: Scribner, 1959.

Freedman, Daniel. "Ethnic Differences in Babies." *HUMAN NATURE*, January 1979.

Freud, Anna. *INFANTS WITHOUT FAMILIES*. New York: International Universities Press, 1944.

Fromm, Erich. *FEAR OF FREEDOM*. London: Routledge & Kegan Paul, Ltd., 1942.

Gardner, Howard. *FRAMES OF MIND: THE THEORY OF MULTIPLE INTELLIGENCES*. New York: Basic Books, 1983.

Gaylin, Willard, M.D. *FEELINGS*. New York: Ballantine Books, 1979.

Gilligan Carol. *IN A DIFFERENT VOICE*. Cambridge: Harvard University Press, 1982.

Ginsburg, H. and Opper, S. *PIAGET'S THEORY OF INTELLECTUAL DEVELOPMENT* (2nd ed.). Englewood Cliffs, N.J.: Prentice-Hall, 1979.

Gould, Roger, "Adult Life Stages: Growth Toward Self Tolerance." *PSYCHOLOGY TODAY*, February 1975, pp. 74-78.

Harlow, H.F. *LEARNING TO LOVE*. New York: Ballantine Books, 1971.

Harlow, H.F. "The Nature of Love." *AMERICAN PSYCHOLOGIST*, 13, 1958, pp. 673-685.

Herron, R.E. and Sutton-Smith, B. *CHILD'S PLAY.* New York: Wiley, 1971.

Horney, Karen. *NEUROSIS AND HUMAN GROWTH.* New York: Norton, 1950.

Horney, Karen. *THE NEUROTIC PERSONALITY OF OUR TIME.* New York: Norton, 1937.

James, John. "Grandparents and the Family Script Parade." *TRANSACTIONAL ANALYSIS JOURNAL,* Vol. 14, No. 1, January 1984, pp. 18-28.

James, Muriel. *MARRIAGE IS FOR LOVING.* Reading, Mass.: Addison-Wesley, 1979.

James, Muriel. "Self-Reparenting: Theory and Process." *TRANSACTIONAL ANALYSIS JOURNAL,* Vol. 4, No. 3, July 1974.

James, Muriel and contributors. *TECHNIQUES IN TRANSACTIONAL ANALYSIS FOR PSYCHOTHERAPISTS AND COUNSELORS.* Reading, Mass.: Addison-Wesley, 1977.

James, Muriel. "Therapy Doesn't Always Hurt: Laugh Therapy." *TRANSACTIONAL ANALYSIS JOURNAL,* Vol. 9, No. 4, October 1979.

James, Muriel. *TRANSACTIONAL ANALYSIS FOR MOMS AND DADS.* Reading, Mass.: Addison-Wesley, 1974.

James, Muriel and Savary, Louis. *A NEW SELF.* Reading, Mass.: Addison-Wesley, 1977.

Kagan, J. *DEVELOPMENTAL STUDIES OF REFLECTION AND ANALYSIS.* Cambridge, Mass.: Harvard University Press, 1964.

Kohlberg, L. and Turiel, E., eds. *RECENT RESEARCH IN MORAL DEVELOPMENT.* New York: Holt, Rinehart & Winston, 1972.

Lamb, M.E., ed. *THE ROLE OF THE FATHER IN CHILD DEVELOPMENT.* New York: Wiley, 1976.

Lazarus, Arnold and Wolpe, Joseph. *BEHAVIOR THERAPY TECHNIQUES.* Oxford: Pergamon Press, 1966.

Leboyer, Frederick. *BIRTH WITHOUT VIOLENCE.* New York: Knopf, 1975.

LeShan, Lawrence. *HOW TO MEDITATE: A GUIDE TO SELF-DISCOVERY.* New York: Bantam Books, 1975.

Lickona, T., ed. *MORAL DEVELOPMENT AND BEHAVIOR: THEORY, RESEARCH, AND SOCIAL ISSUES.* New York: Holt, Rinehart & Winston, 1976.

Lynd, Helen Merrill. *ON SHAME AND THE SEARCH FOR IDENTITY.* New York: Science Editions, 1966.

Madruga, Lenor. *ONE STEP AT A TIME.* New York: McGraw-Hill, 1979.

Maier, Henry. *THREE THEORIES OF CHILD DEVELOPMENT.* New York: Harper & Row, 1965.

Maslow, Abraham. *THE FURTHER REACHES OF HUMAN NATURE.* New York: Viking, 1972.

Maslow, Abraham. *MOTIVATION AND PERSONALITY* (2nd ed.). Princeton, N.J.: D. Van Nostrand Co., 1968.

Maslow, Abraham. *TOWARD A PSYCHOLOGY OF BEING* (2nd ed.). Princeton, N.J.: D. Van Nostrand Co., 1968.

Masterson, James F., M.D. *THE NARCISSISTIC AND BORDERLINE DISORDERS: AN INTEGRATED DEVELOPMENTAL APPROACH.* New York: Brunner/Mazel, 1981.

Milgram, Stanley. *OBEDIENCE TO AUTHORITY.* New York: Harper & Row, 1974.

Miller, N. and Dollard, J. *SOCIAL LEARNING AND IMITATION.* New Haven: Yale University Press, 1941.

Montagu, Ashley. "Constitutional and Prenatal Factors in Infant and Child Health." In *HUMAN DEVELOPMENT,* Morris Haimowitz and Natalie Haimowitz, eds., 3rd ed. New York: Thomas Crowell Co., 1973.

Montagu, Ashley. *LIFE BEFORE BIRTH.* New York: New American Library, Signet Books, 1965.

Moody, Raymond, Jr. *LAUGH AFTER LAUGH.* Jacksonville, Fla.: Headwaters Press, 1978.

Piaget, Jean. *THE CONSTRUCTION OF REALITY IN THE CHILD.* New York: Basic Books, 1954.

Piaget, Jean. *THE MORAL JUDGEMENT OF THE CHILD.* New York: Harcourt, Brace, 1932; Collier Books Edition, 1962.

Rokeach, Milton. *THE NATURE OF HUMAN VALUES.* New York: Free Press, 1973.

Selye, Hans. *STRESS WITHOUT DISTRESS.* Philadelphia: J.B. Lippincott, 1974.

Sheehy, Gail. *PASSAGES: PREDICTABLE CRISES IN ADULT LIFE.* New York: E.P. Dutton, 1976.

Simonton, O. Carl, M.D.; Matthews-Simonton, Stephanie; and Creighton, James. *GETTING WELL AGAIN.* Los Angeles: J.P. Tarcher, Inc., 1978.

Sorokin, Pitirim A. *THE WARP AND POWER OF LOVE.* Chicago: Henry Regnery, 1967.

Spitz, R.A. *THE FIRST YEAR OF LIFE.* New York: International Universities Press, 1965.

Stern, D. *THE FIRST RELATIONSHIP: MOTHER AND INFANT.* Cambridge, Mass.: Harvard University Press, 1977.

Sullivan, Harry Stack. *THE FUSION OF PSYCHIATRY AND SOCIAL SCIENCE.* New York: W.W. Norton, 1964.

Tavris, Carol. *ANGER: THE MISUNDERSTOOD EMOTION.* New York: Simon & Schuster, Inc., a Touchstone Book, 1982.

Terman, L.M. and Oden, M. *GENETIC STUDIES OF GENIUS: THE GIFTED GROUP AT MIDLIFE. THIRTY-FIVE YEARS FOLLOWUP OF THE SUPERIOR CHILD.* Stanford, Calif.: Stanford University Press, 1954.

Theobald, Robert. *HABIT AND HABITAT.* Princeton, N.J.: Prentice Hall, 1972.

Thomas, Alexander, and Chess, Stella. *TEMPERAMENT AND DEVELOPMENT.* New York: Brunner/Mazel, 1977.

Thomas, Alexander; Chess, Stella; and Birch, Herbert G. *TEMPERAMENT AND BEHAVIOR DISORDERS IN CHILDREN.* New York: New York University Press, 1969.

United Nations. *A HANDBOOK OF ITS STRUCTURE AND ACTIVITIES,* 9th ed. New York: United Nations, 1980.

Winnicott, D.W. *PLAYING AND REALITY.* London: Tavistock Publications Ltd., 1971.

Index